Thailand

- A in the text denotes a highly recommended sight
- A complete A–Z of practical information starts on p.103
- Extensive mapping on cover flaps and in text

Berlitz Publishing Company, Inc.

Princeton   Mexico City   Dublin   Eschborn   Singapore

Text:	Ben Davies
Editors:	Jane Middleton, Donald Greig
Photography:	Ben Davies
Layout:	Media Content Marketing, Inc.
Cartography:	🌐 Falk-Verlag, Munich

Thanks to the Tourist Authority of Thailand (TAT) for their invaluable assistance in the preparation of this guide.

Found an error we should know about? Our editor would be happy to hear from you, and a postcard would do. Although we make every effort to ensure the accuracy of all the information in this book, changes do occur.

ISBN 2-8315-6358-5
Revised 1998 – Second Printing December 1998

Printed in Switzerland by Weber SA, Bienne
029/812 RP

CONTENTS

THAILAND

THAILAND AND THE THAIS

Thailand infuses all the colour and excitement of the Far East with its own particular charm. From its glittering temples and smiling people to palm-lined beaches and shady hideaways, it has more to offer than just about any other destination in the world. Colourful markets, villages on stilts, and exotic national parks where elephants run wild are among its attractions; even the monolithic new cities are filled with an irresistible blend of Western and Asian allure.

Bigger than Spain, but a bit smaller than France, Thailand is more than spacious enough to be home to all the scenery you could imagine. Its tallest peak, near Chiang Mai in the north, is a respectable height of about 2,590 metres (8,500 feet). On the central plain around Bangkok, however, the landscape of paddy fields, rivers, and canals is as flat and green as a billiard table. Over 70 percent of the population is involved in rice farming, not to mention several million water buffalo, too.

Thailand's climate, which is officially classified as tropical monsoon, is best enjoyed from November to February, when the relatively cool, dry air rolls down from China to the north, reducing Bangkok's temperatures from scorching to merely hot. In the northern hills, you might even find yourself wanting a sweater after sundown. Between May and October, the southwest monsoon alternates deluges with rainbows.

No matter when you reach Bangkok, the main commercial and political centre, you should be ready for heat, pollution, and sheer chaos. This is a place that was once known as the Venice of the East, with canals crisscrossing the somnolent, riverine streets. Nowadays, although the old way of life

> **Do not touch anyone on the head, which is considered sacred.**

There is a little piece of sand for everybody in Phuket, the pearl of Thailand's tourist industry and the largest island in the kingdom.

still exists along the waterways, you are more likely to find massive traffic jams and high-rise buildings.

Estimates of the population of Bangkok stand at around eight million people, or 12 percent of the entire country—a figure that continues to grow in leaps and bounds—and the city contains over one million cars and eleven thousand restaurants. Even here, however, amidst all the chaos, there are things that are uniquely Thai, from chanting Buddhist monks and bustling marketplaces to spirit houses heaped with colourful orchids and lotus blossoms.

Over 90 percent of the population is Buddhist, and both the religion and the philosophy of Buddhism permeate all facets of national life. Founded in India, Buddhism first came to Thailand in 303 B.C., when it thrived as the religion of kings and as a unifier of the people. To see Buddhism in practice today, you will not have to go very far. At dawn, even in the capital, you will see monks

> **On being introduced, Thais will place both palms together beneath their chin, fingers pointing upwards.**

on the early-morning alms round. Those lucky enough to be present at an ordination ceremony in a temple witness the most magnificent sight of all: saffron-robed novices being carried high above the shoulders of friends and family.

Monks are not the only outward sign of the religion that, along with the monarchy, has given strength and continuity to the kingdom. Great temples offered to Buddha are everywhere; the Grand Palace or the Wat Arun shouldn't be missed in Bangkok, or, farther afield, the magnificent ruins of Sukhothai or Ayutthaya.

If you prefer more natural attractions, head for one of the vast national parks, which now constitute a huge 34,500 square km (13,320 square miles) portion of Thailand. Of particular note

A day's work for two Yao village women.

is Khao Yai park because of its birdlife and waterfalls. Iridescent kingfishers and orange-breasted, red-headed trogons flit beneath the shade of leafy canopies. Gibbons and flying squirrels, elephants, black bears, and tigers dwell in these vast stretches of dense evergreen. You might catch a glimpse of any one of over 900 different species. Orchids grow in abundance, and there is a multitude of butterflies.

Farther south, if you want underwater adventure, cruise to beautiful Ko Phi Phi, or explore the long, lazy beaches at famous Phuket and Ko Samui.

More unspoilt are the arid plains of Isaan in the northeast —or, alternatively, trek among the hill people of the Golden Triangle up north, where poppies have earned it a reputation as one of the world's largest opium-producing regions.

Don't miss the opportunity of a trip on the Mekong, either. One of the world's great rivers, it runs down from Tibet, irrigating the rice fields in the north of Thailand before it empties out in the Nam Khong Delta of South Vietnam.

A saffron-robed monk finds a moment to read a newspaper.

However, it is the people, even more so than the sights and scenery, who often afford the most memorable experiences. From friendly northerners to the rice farmers in the central plains, the philosophy underlying every aspect of life is simply *mai pen rai* (literally "no worries"). Such a relaxed attitude has its roots partly in Thailand's history, for unlike almost all the rest of

Southeast Asia, Thailand was never subject to European power, so resentment towards foreigners has never festered. Thailand translates as "Land of the Free," and the Thai people take pride in their past and in their constitutional monarchy, both of which are significant to uniting the country.

The figures of one census put the population of Thailand at 55 million, over 70 percent of whom inhabit the countryside. Not everyone is of pure Thai stock, and it is estimated that as many as 3 million residents are descendants of migrants from Burma, Laos, and Cambodia who came to Thailand hundreds of years ago.

An Akha village boy in tribal wear.

Economically, the Thais are emerging as a major industrial nation. Although 60 percent of the population still farm the land, producing over 22 million tons of rice each year and enabling Thailand to remain the world's chief exporter of tinned pineapple, the country also exports significant volumes of textiles, electronics, and jewellery.

Not that work is allowed to interfere with play. Thais love the good things in life, a fact that is clear from their enjoyment of Thai food, which is on a par with French and Chi-

nese as one of the world's classic cuisines. Typical flavours and tastes are spicy, sour, hot, and sweet, and the success of these dishes often relies on delightful contrasts which ensure the palate never becomes jaded. Delicacies such as prawns in coconut, or succulent chicken wrapped in a banana leaf, take their place amongst an array of culinary specialities. Indeed, it would probably be possible to enjoy a different type of dish every day of your visit and still leave plenty untasted.

Just the thing to work up an appetite for feasting is a visit to the shops and markets, for Thailand ranks as one of Southeast Asia's finest shopping destinations. As you walk through the markets keep your eyes open for beautifully woven baskets, or for the silk that is famous worldwide, due to its quality. If you're in the north, go in search of colourful umbrellas—you can watch while they're being painted—and wherever you are, don't overlook traditional wooden carvings (but don't be taken in by more modern imitations, either, which are usually less attractive, and not always cheaper).

At Wat Benchamabophit: the mythical maga snake that raised Buddha to heaven guards many temple entrances.

A BRIEF HISTORY

Recent archaeological finds in northeast Thailand (formerly Siam) are turning traditional ideas on their head. Relics discovered in the village of Ban Chiang dating back over 5,000 years are still being studied, but seem to prove that Thailand was home to one of the first Bronze Age civilizations, predating that of China.

What happened to the prehistoric people is not known. As for the Thais, it is probable that they did not reach the area until the 11th or 12th centuries. According to anthropologists, they then spread south across vast areas of the fertile Chao Phraya valley, at the same time displacing both the Mons and Khmers. Around A.D. 1259, the kingdom of Lanna (Land of a Million Rice Fields) was established in what is now northern Thailand. Chiang Rai was chosen as capital to start with, but when King Mengrai spotted five white mice, two white sambars, and two white barking deer together on the banks of the Ping River, he relocated the capital to Chiang Mai.

Mengrai ruled prosperously until the age of 80, when he was struck by lightning. (Later kings died in even more surprising ways, like King Kamphoo, whose brief reign ended in 1345 when he was devoured by a crocodile. In more recent times, in 1946, Rama VIII, the brother of the present king of Thailand, was found shot dead in bed. The mystery of his death remains unsolved.)

Dawn of Happiness

The first great chapter of Thai history began with King Ramkamhaeng the Great, the ruler of Sukhothai (founded at some time in the 1230s) from about 1280 to 1317. Ramkamhaeng—who was renowned for legendary exploits on elephants—managed to nurture a powerful kingdom and a

Ayutthaya: ruins of one of the greatest civilizations that reigned in Thailand.

thriving haven for the arts. In its heyday, the kingdom stretched from Lampang in the north of Thailand to Vientiane, now part of Laos, and south towards the Malay Peninsula. Many scholars say that the first Thai alphabet derives from this period. Sukhothai contributed some of the finest examples of Thai sculpture in history, many of which can still be viewed in parts of the old city today.

However, after the death of King Ramkamhaeng, the kingdom's power declined. By the 15th century the city was little more than a provincial town, and shortly afterwards it was abandoned altogether.

Ayutthaya

Sukhothai's downfall cleared the way for what was to be an even greater kingdom. Established in 1350, Ayutthaya continued for over 400 years and earned a place as one of the East's greatest civilizations.

Under King U-Thong and a succession of legendary monarchs, the kingdom expanded rapidly. Towards the end of the 14th century, the Khmers were driven out of vast areas of central and northern Thailand, and the people of Sukhothai were finally vanquished. In 1431 the capital at Angkor in Cambodia was sacked, and Ayutthaya's pre-eminence was established beyond question.

Ayutthaya became a centre for trade between China, India, and Europe, in which teak and spices were bartered for gold and for cannon, which the Siamese pulled behind their elephants.

In spite of the loss of several kings—who were either cudgelled to death or poisoned—the people of Ayutthaya were, by all accounts, a happy lot, "much given to pleasure and ryot" according to the observations of one 17th-century traveller. Opium was in abundant supply, and cohabitation and wife-swapping found enthusiastic supporters.

Most foreigners who came to Ayutthaya during the 17th century were impressed by the sheer size and opulence of the Siamese capital. Directors of the East India Company compared it favourably with London, estimating its population to be anything from 300,000 to 1 million. With palaces, canals, and temples, the city acquired a justified reputation of being the most beautiful in Asia.

European influence reached its zenith during the reign of King Narai (1657–1688), when the courts of Siam were visited by ambassadors from as far away as the court of Louis XIV, along with explorers, zealous Jesuit missionaries, and traders. One Greek adventurer, named Geraki Constantine Phaulkon, was even appointed the king's first minister, and acted as the principal go-between when diplomatic exchanges were held.

Such promotion inevitably sparked jealousy, however, and shortly before the king died in 1688 Phaulkon was executed after being arrested at the time of a bloody revolt. After this incident, Thailand had almost no contact with the West for the following 150 years.

A serene statue of Buddha at a temple in Lamphun reflects the tranquility of this ancient town.

Between the 15th and 18th centuries, the Thais fought innumerable battles against the neighbouring Burmese. A consequence of this was the conflict of April 1767, when after a 14-month siege, the Burmese succeeded in capturing Ayutthaya. They pillaged the city and vandalized every aspect of Thai culture and art. The sack of Ayutthaya, a great tragedy in Thai history, still casts a shadow over the national consciousness of the Thai people.

One survivor, a young general from Tak province, rallied the remnants of the Thai army and managed to expel the Burmese garrison. Ayutthaya had been almost totally destroyed, however, so Taksin—as he was known—founded a new capital at Thon Buri, directly across the Chao Phraya river from what has since become Bangkok. Though his father was actually Chinese—and a commoner at that—Taksin was crowned King of Thailand. He ruled until 1782, at which point he was dethroned on the grounds of madness and ceremoniously executed with a club of scented sandalwood.

From Thon Buri to Bangkok

With the death of Taksin, there rose to power the first king of the Chakris Dynasty, the greatest in Thai history, which still populates the throne today.

Rama I immediately moved his capital from Thon Buri to Bangkok on the east bank of the river, saying that the new city would be larger and easier to defend. He then went on to defeat a number of marauding Burmese expeditions.

His son, Rama II, devoted himself to preserving Thai literature, and produced a classic version of the Thai *Ramayana* or *Ramakien*, the epic Sanskrit poem. He also re-established relations with the West, and still found time to sire 73 children by 38 mothers.

Although no less influential, Rama III (1824–1851) is largely overlooked by historians. As a devout Buddhist he built some of Bangkok's finest temples, including Wat Arun

Kings Rule
When it came to rhetorical flourishes, the monarchs of Ayutthaya in the 17th century took the biscuit. Any mortal who was so bold as to address the king was obliged to start as follows: "High and mighty Lord of me, thy slave, I desire to take thy royal word and put it in my brain and on the top of my head." Those who failed to follow this code of conduct were summarily chastised with bamboos. Others were buried alive in the cement walls surrounding the city.

and parts of Wat Pho. He also went on to introduce Western medicine to his country—including smallpox vaccinations —as well as arranging for American missionaries to visit, one of whom brought the first printing press with Thai type.

The King and I

The most renowned of all the early monarchs is, lamentably, better known for his excessive libido than his actual achievements. King Mongkut, a Buddhist monk for 27 years, took 35 wives by whom he had 83 children. He was depicted as a cruel, frivolous despot in the memoirs of court tutor Anna Leonowens, which later provided the basis for *The King and I*. This reputation has saddened the Thais, who still worship Mongkut as one of the greatest and most progressive monarchs. Not only was he a man of considerable sophistication, he was also better educated than the kings of Europe. He could speak seven foreign languages, including Latin and English, and was an expert in astronomy. It was during his reign that commoners were allowed for the first time to set eyes on the King of Siam, waterways and roads were built, and laws set down to improve rights for women and children.

Mongkut was succeeded by Rama V, who became known as Chulalongkorn, or Lord of the White Elephant, and was one of the most popular and enlightened of all the kings. During his 42-year reign, he abolished slavery and established a schooling system, the first post office, and a national library. He led his country literally as well as symbolically into the 20th century—and is still remembered with considerable affection today.

The World Wars

The effect of World War I was to propel Thailand out of isolation. In 1917, King Vajiravudh (Rama VI) dispatched

This dragon in Thailand's Chinatown is more than a flash of beautiful colours—it represents the path to heaven's gate.

troops to France to support the Allied cause. A likely explanation for his sympathies is that he was Cambridge educated and had served for a time in the British army. Once the war was over, Siam became a member of the League of Nations.

One legacy of Rama VI was surnames for the Thai people. Prior to the war, family names were not used in Siam, but the king decreed that all his subjects adopt one. Women were encouraged to grow their hair long like Western women, and even football was introduced, with a Royal team.

The genteel world of Siam was rocked once more in 1932, when a group of army officers staged a bloodless revolution which brought the monarchy's absolute supremacy to an end.

The authorities of Siam (by then renamed Thailand) signed friendship agreements with the Japanese in 1940. The

*Warriors are depicted in this stone carving
of the ancient capitol of Angkor Wat.*

following year, the Japanese invaded Thailand, and soon afterwards the Thais, seeing resistance as hopeless, entered World War II on the side of the Axis. Despite the fact that Thailand was on the losing side, it was later able to join the

United Nations due to a legal loophole in the original declaration of war.

Since 1932, continual political turbulence has beset Thailand. The country has endured 17 coups, while over 31 prime ministers have been appointed, none of whom has lasted a full term. Ironically though, Thailand is deemed one of the most stable countries in a part of the world which until recently was regarded as extremely volatile. It sided with the United States during the Vietnam War, and throughout its history it has remained resolutely anti-communist and pro-monarchy.

Even now, however, the balance is uncertain. In May 1992 more than 100 pro-democracy demonstrators were wounded by the military in the wake of massive protests that called for the resignation of non-elected Prime Minister Suchinda Kraprayoon. These events jolted the country to the brink of chaos and were only resolved by the intervention of King Bhumipol, the reigning monarch, who advocated reconciliation amongst the different parties. Although a stable, democratically elected government has since taken over, the events of May 1992 serve as a reminder of the past and of the uncertain political future that still overshadows Thailand.

Coup de Grâce

Of all the attempted military coups in Thailand (17 in total), that which took place in 1950 must be recorded as one of the most bizarre. In May of that year, Prime Minister Phibul Song-khram was forced at gunpoint onto a naval ship moored in the Chao Phraya River. Negotiations failed to break the deadlock, and loyal forces launched an air and ground attack on the vessel. Fearing for the safety of their respected hostage, Phibul's captors helped him to swim to shore. Once there he telephoned headquarters, was picked up, and returned to power intact.

WHERE TO GO

BANGKOK

Thailand's capital might well come as a shock to the senses, but there is plenty to see for anyone prepared to put up with the heat and confusion. From its huge shopping malls, shady temples, and bustling markets to its restaurants, sleepy canals, and brazen nightlife, Bangkok offers endless surprises. King Rama I modelled the city on Ayutthaya, with its canals that crisscross the city and its magnificent temples. Much of the old town has been replaced by the bursting metropolis which extends on all sides, but there are still beautiful temples as well as palaces, historic buildings, and, of course, Bangkok's notorious nightclubs.

The great distances and the heat make it one of the world's least walkable cities, and aimless sauntering may result in nothing but a twisted ankle, for the pavements are chronically torn up. Three preferable options are to find yourself a taxi, a *tuk-tuk* (three-wheeled motorbike scooter), or a coach tour, which can be arranged in any hotel. Ideas—in addition to a selection of leaflets—on what to do are given by the Tourism Authority of Thailand (T.A.T.) on Bamrung Muang Road.

It is worth remembering that pleasure in Bangkok is usually equal to effort—the more you put into the place, the more you'll enjoy it; and those who do take the time and trouble will discover one of the great capitals of the East.

Major Districts

Before you set out to explore the city, buy a map. Only with an extremely detailed and up-to-date city plan will you be able to take on the unplanned chaos that is Bangkok. What's more, don't expect to find a town centre, for the city's sights are widely spread, with several major districts vying for attention. Start your tour with the greatest monuments, and head for the area called **Royal Bangkok**, which is situated just a stone's throw from the Chao Phraya River that runs through the city. This is the oldest part of the city, and is home to Wat Arun and Wat Pho, as well as the magnificent Grand Palace (see page 25).

To the south is one of Bangkok's original shopping centres. The **New Road** (which is also known as Charoen Krung Road) runs around the General Post Office and was the first official road in Thailand. This area is still well supplied with gift shops and "instant" tailors. Several churches and embassies are situated between Charoen Krung and the river, as is the celebrated Oriental Hotel, once the haunt of such figures as Joseph Conrad, Noel Coward, and Somerset Maugham.

Life along the Chao Phraya River that runs through Bangkok.

You may not find celebrities in **Chinatown** (the lively district off Charoen Krung), but you will see a profusion of entrepreneurs. Take a walk along Soi Wanit (formerly known as Sampeng Lane), with its shops selling Chinese lanterns, wigs, sharkfin soup, and gold necklaces. You can follow it up with a visit to the busy markets which are held at Ratchawong and Yaowarat roads.

> Most taxis have no meters and a price must be agreed with the driver before tha ride begins.

Cinemas, cafés, restaurants, and boutiques populate **Siam Square**, a low-rise grid of shopping arcades and streets fashionable with the young, with four- and five-storey air-conditioned shopping centres alongside. Keep an eye open for the city's most important spirit house on the corner of Rajadamri Road and Ploenchit Road. The **Erawan Shrine** was built by the owners of the former Erawan Hotel following various

Thailand's ancient ideals meet modern ordeals in the bustling city of Bangkok.

mishaps, the final straw being the sinking at sea of a ship bringing marble to the hotel. There have been no further incidents since the shrine was finished, and today a steady stream of the faithful arrive to offer flowers, boiled eggs, and bottles of whisky to the resident spirits.

Farther east, across the railway tracks, Ploenchit Road becomes **Sukhumvit Road**. This marks the start of a rambling shopping, entertainment, and residential area; be warned if you are trying to find somewhere specific, though, for all the side roads (*sois*) have numbers as opposed to names, and wherever you go it is imperative that you have the full numerical address.

A final area to contend with lies to the south, along Silom Road. This is home to the business district and to the best-known street of all: **Patpong**, that small plot of land which started as a rice terrace and is now possibly the most famous red-light district in the world.

The Grand Palace

If you have time for only one sight in Bangkok, then make it the Grand Palace, the fabulous city within a city which is situated a short stroll to the east of the river, near the Tha Chang pier. Begun in 1782 during the reign of King Rama I, and refined and enlarged by successive Chakri monarchs, this 2½-sq-km (1-square-mile) area has been transformed into an incomparable fairytale world of jewel-encrusted monuments and spires.

Make sure you allow at least a couple of hours—enough to give you a sense of the place—and don't forget that flipflops and shorts are banned; respectful dress is required.

A pair of 200-year-old lions—Chinese stone sculptures—stand fiercely before the gate leading to the **Audience Hall of Dusit Maha Prasad**. These statues are said to have reached Bangkok as ballast on Chinese junks fetching Thai rice.

Bangkok's best-known monument—the Grand Palace.
More gold is added every year to ensure it keeps its shine.

The current Dusit Hall was built in 1789 on the site of an earlier building that was struck by lightning. Although not the original, it has a traditional gilded, nine-tier roof supported by four *garudas* (large mythical birds), which are clasping dragon-headed serpents.

On the edge of the square, near the Hall, you will see an elegant white-marble building known as the Disrobing Pavilion. This was where the king would alight from his carriage and adjust his ceremonial hat before entering the throne hall.

Even more impressive is the **Chakri Mahaprasad**, which is the centrepiece of the whole complex. It was built by the internationally minded Rama V, and blends Asian and Italian Renaissance styles. Of particular note are the central balcony and approach stairway. These are topped by a traditional roof which rises in stages to three seven-tiered spires. Below the central spire stands a golden urn which contains the ashes of the Chakri kings.

To the east is the **Audience Hall of Amarindra**. Built during the reign of Rama I, it contains two thrones, the upper in the shape of a boat, the lower covered by a magnificent nine-tiered white canopy.

Among all this "King and I" architecture, one palace in particular stands out above all the others. **Wat Phra Kaeo**, the royal chapel and Temple of the Emerald Buddha, is covered in finery unrivalled by anything or anywhere else in Thailand, protected by a nine-tiered umbrella, and surrounded by gold murals. The Emerald Buddha itself stands just 75 centimetres (30 inches) tall and is made of jade. Thais believe that so long as it remains in their hands, Thailand will be safe. Such is the veneration for the Emerald Buddha that each season the king himself dresses the image in different robes: gilded gold and sapphires in the rainy season, a diamond robe for summer, and woven saffron in winter.

Inside the royal chapel, photography and shoes are forbidden—you'll be reminded to take off your shoes outside. As you sit on the floor, take in the grandeur of the scene, but remember to make sure (here as in all temples) that your feet do not point towards the altar. It is considered disrespectful.

On the way out you can also visit the modestly named **Coin Museum**. Displayed in glass cases in two jail-like enclaves are gold coins, swords, and crown jewels, all dating from the 11th century.

Six Great Wats

Visit six of Bangkok's *wats*—monasteries or temples—as part of your tour of its greatest architectural wonders, but do make sure that you leave plenty of time, as distances between them can be quite considerable.

One of the best-known landmarks, the splendid **Wat Arun** (Temple of Dawn), stands on the opposite bank of the Chao Phraya River in Thon Buri, but is only a minute or two away by ferry. The temple was built during the first half of the 19th century by Rama II and Rama III, and is decorated with millions of fragments of porcelain arranged in the shape of flowers. The central tower is taller than a 20-storey building and affords stunning views across the river—but the stairs are steep and the exit narrow. Photographers and

> It is not appropriate to enter a temple in shorts or very informal clothing, and you will be asked to remove your shoes.

What's a Wat?

Although you will see *wats*, or Buddhist temples, everywhere in Thailand, you may find it something of a problem coming to grips with their specialized vocabulary. Here's a brief rundown of the most common architectural terms:

bot: main sanctuary of a temple where religious rites are held

chedi: bell-like dome, often containing holy relics

chofa: graceful ornament extending from the roof

prang: cylinder with rounded top, pointing up like a finger

stupa: tower or pagoda, often a burial site

viharn: hall of worship or for preaching

anyone not so appreciative of heights will do better to sit on the opposite bank of the river at sunset.

Wat Pho, Bangkok's oldest monastery, houses an incredible 16th-century gilt reclining Buddha in its vast white enclosure. Almost 15 metres (49 feet) high and 46 metres (151 feet) long, it reaches right up to the roof of the temple. On the feet, inlaid with mother-of-pearl, are the 108 auspicious characteristics of the Buddha.

A tall teak structure painted red and called the Giant Swing stands incongruously outside the monastery of **Wat Suthat**. In former years, death-defying swingers used to show off their ac-

Bangkok's Wat Benchamabophit — the marble temple is one of the finest examples of recent religious architecture in the city.

robatic skills during the annual Brahmin harvest festival. The show has not been held since 1935, however, when it was stopped after several of the faithful lost their balance. Don't miss one of Bangkok's most beautiful (and largest) Buddhas at the temple nearby. Outside, graceful bronze horses stand at the four corners of the building.

Wat Saket, better known as the Golden Mount, can be seen long before you reach it. It sits atop Bangkok's only hill —and an artificial one at that—surmounted by a big gold *chedi* (dome). Spiral steps up the mount's reinforced sides lead to a viewing platform. Take a map with you to identify the palaces and temples spread out below. The faithful make the climb less for the view than for the shrine containing relics of the Buddha. These were given to King Rama V in 1897 by Lord Curzon, viceroy of India.

The best time to visit **Wat Benchamabophit**, the Marble Temple, is at dawn, when the graceful marble is still tinged with orange and the monks are queueing for their daily alms. Built at the turn of the century, it is thought to be the finest instance of recent temple architecture in the city. It is a haven of calm, with its inner courtyard surrounded by statues of the Buddha, and its ponds filled with plump fish and turtles, fed daily with papaya and bananas by the monks and other believers. Outside and past the canal are the monks' quarters, set amongst green lawns.

The impressive Buddha at **Wat Traimit** might have remained concealed forever had it not been for workmen extending the port of Bangkok, who dropped the then stucco-covered statue from a crane, revealing the vast Buddha inside. This is Thailand's largest gold image, weighing 4½ metric tons (5 tons) and dating from the Sukhothai period, when it was probably disguised to keep it out of the hands of the warring Burmese.

Museums and Palaces

On Na Phra That Road, a short walk from the Grand Palace, the **National Museum** houses Thailand's finest collection of antiquities. The sculpture, ceramics, and jewellery here offer insight into the country's unique synthesis of different cultures—as well as the sheer variety of the kingdom's artefacts. Try to be there for a tour (ask at Tourism Authority offices for times) lest you be overwhelmed by the size and scope of the place.

The earliest works—from excavations at Ban Chiang in northeast Thailand—are the most interesting: pots and jars with bold designs in the shape of fingerprints. The haunting patterns are curiously modern, and yet the pottery is probably 5,000 years old.

The museum exhibition divides Thai culture into several periods, starting off with the Dvaravati (A.D. sixth–11th centuries), then tracing the development of political power to Lan Na, Sukhothai, Ayutthaya, and ultimately Bangkok (late 18th-century to present-day art is also known as Ratanakosin). As you go through the rooms, arranged chronologically, you can see the changes in the portrayal of the Buddha, the overriding theme of Thai art.

The National Museum in Bangkok houses Thailand's finest collection of antiquities.

The museum offers a range of other things to see, from an 18-metric-ton (20-ton) royal funeral chariot—which needed over 290 people to push it—to thrones, litters, 19th-century Thai typewriters, and even a full-sized model elephant fitted out for battle.

A different sort of museum is situated in the magnificent edifice known as **Jim Thompson's house**, located to the east of the city off a smelly little canal. Bringing a sense of calm to even the most frenetic of days, the cool timber rooms of this teak house (open Monday to Friday) are packed with priceless artefacts, sculptures, and ceramics.

The story of Jim Thompson is as intriguing as his taste in art. A New York architect, he came to Southeast Asia as a secret agent in World War II. Settling in Bangkok after the war, he converted the Thai silk industry from a primitive craft into international big business. In 1967 he vanished while on holiday in neighbouring Malaysia. The mystery is still unsolved. No trace of Thompson has ever been found, but this monument, "the house on the *klong*" (canal), is as he left it.

The huge palace known as **Vimanmek** (Celestial Residence) might lack mystery, but it's certainly not short of scale. It was built during the reign of King Chulalongkorn, is reputed to be the largest teak building in the world, and contains an impressive collection of objets d'art, paintings, and royal jewellery, plus the first shower ever installed in Thailand. Recently restored under the patronage of Queen Sirikit, the palace is now open daily.

One final building not to be missed is the **Suan Pakkard Palace** on Sri Ayutthaya Road. This superb building is owned by Princess Chumbot and surrounded by leafy gardens that are home to a gruff but friendly pelican. Down at the bottom of the impeccable garden stands the delightful Lacquer Pavilion, which is believed to be the only house of its type to survive the sack of Ayutthaya in 1767. Bought in 1959, the pavilion was then rebuilt here as a gift to the princess from her late husband. Some of the inside walls are covered with exquisite paintings—gold leaf on black lacquer—which illustrate scenes in the life of the Buddha and episodes from the national legend, the *Ramakien*. Suan Pakkard (which literally translates as "lettuce garden") is open daily except Sunday.

Bangkok Afloat

The most popular way of exploring the fascinating *klongs* (canals), which are so central to Bangkok's character, is to take either a tour from Tha Chang pier near the Grand Palace, or a similar trip arranged by any of the hotels. A one-hour tour (including a visit to the snake farm; see page 35) is quite expensive, but will take you to sections of old Thon Buri that you would hardly dream still existed—past floating restaurants and petrol (gasoline) stations, old wooden houses, and temples.

Most river tours leave early in the morning and include a visit to the **royal barges** in their shed in Klong Bangkok Noi. All the ceremonial craft are like dreamboats come true —otherworldly vessels trimmed with fanciful prows and elaborate red and gold decorations. The king's own boat is propelled by 50 oarsmen.

You can explore the canals on your own by means of the local shuttle boats, long-tailed *hang yaos*. These long, narrow craft, powered by noisy truck engines, carry the propellor on the end of a long drive shaft—hence their name, "long-tailed" boats. You can also hire your own *hang yao* by the hour, but as with taxis, be sure to agree on a price in advance.

Down Klong Bangkok Noi (Small Canal) and Klong Yai (Big Canal), handsome houses with gardens and fountains are squashed cheek by jowl with old, wooden houses on

stilts, shaded by palm trees. Nearby you will see rubber tyre factories and temples, floating supermarkets and snack bars.

Anyone who prefers slower and cheaper transport can take one of the public water taxis known as Chao Phraya Express Boats that travel up and down the river at regular 20-minute intervals. If you start either at the landing alongside the Oriental Hotel, or Tha Chang pier near the Grand Palace, you can spend 90 minutes passing by some of Bangkok's greatest monuments, although you will have to get off at Nonthaburi, which is the end of the line. Be warned, though: getting a seat is not always that easy, and a lengthy stand in the heat can be a painful experience.

At Nonthaburi, a small market is the main point of interest. The last boats return at 6:00 P.M., after which you can only take a more expensive taxi.

Diversions

Bored of temples? Fed up with museums and canals? Then try one of the following:

Chatuchak Market. Don't forget to bring your camera to Chatuchak, for this is the most extensive and mind-numbing collection of stalls that you can imagine. Anything from wigs to potted plants and herbal cures for insomnia is available. Take note, though: Chatuchak opens on Saturday and Sunday only, from dawn to dusk.

Snake farm. At the Pasteur Institute, where Henri Durant and Rama IV roads meet, venomous, striped, banded kraits are the pick of the bunch. All the wriggling specimens here are owned by Thailand's Red Cross, which supplies medical centres throughout the kingdom with snakebite serum. The

Floating markets like Damnoen Saduak have almost become a thing of the past.

deadly snakes are milked for humanity—and visitor interest
—every morning at 11:00.

Dusit Zoo. The Thais themselves don't come to Dusit Zoo
to see the wildlife in its natural habitat, but to watch elephants and deer beg for food. In the off-colour pond, where
romantic couples go boating, giant turtles even try to con-
sume Coca-Cola bottles. Apart from the animals and ad-
mirably landscaped aviary, the zoo is probably the best place
in Bangkok just to watch the Thai people having fun. Open
every day.

Lumpini Park. Lumpini is a relative haven of peace in
the city centre. Thais come here at the weekend to picnic and
indulge in the art of *sanuk* (good time). In addition to stalls
selling kebabs and noodles, at the park's northern exit (leading to Soi Sarasin) there is a bar and restaurant from where
you can watch the sun go down.

AROUND BANGKOK

The following excursions are all easily reached from Bangkok, and make rewarding side trips or useful stepping stones
on the way north or south.

West of Bangkok

Rose Garden and Nakhon Pathom

One hour's drive to the west of Bangkok's heat and tumult
lies the cool and calm Rose Garden. The roses constitute
only a small part of 20 hectares (49 acres) of blissful tropical gardens. A cultural performance is staged daily at 3:00
P.M. featuring folk and classical dances, sword fights, Thai
boxing, and a traditional Thai wedding. In addition you can
take a ride on an elephant or even be photographed wrapped
up in a monstrously long, but guaranteed "tame" python.

From the Rose Garden, continue 30 km (20 miles) west to Nakhon Pathom (widely believed to be Thailand's oldest town), home to the biggest *chedi* in the country. King Mongkut built the pagoda, which resembles an upside-down ice-cream cone, in the middle of the 19th century on top of the ruins of an ancient temple dating back over 1,000 years. During the 1970s, this new *chedi* almost collapsed, but fortunately the Fine Arts Department took prompt action and saved the day, so now it can still be seen in all its glory.

Also at Nakhon Pathom is the **Sanam Chan Palace**. This modern structure is entirely in traditional Thai style, with the exception of an English Tudor building, which was once used as a setting for Shakespeare plays.

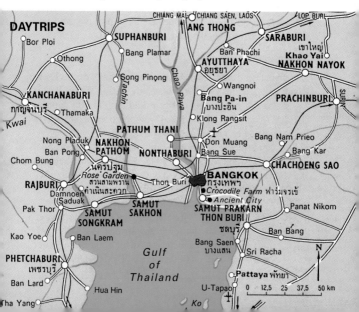

☞ *Floating Market*

You won't need a guide to take you to the floating market at **Damnoen Saduak**—everyone is running tours there nowadays. Nonetheless, the diminutive boats piled with coconuts, bananas, and durian remain as authentic as ever—almost.

Try to get there early, while the women in broad-brimmed hats are out in full force, paddling along the narrow canals and haggling for a bunch of chillies or barbecued fish. Photographers might want to walk along the edge of the canal, or stop on the wooden bridges, which make excellent spots for observing. For a few hundred baht a boat can even be arranged to paddle you out into the centre of the fray.

At another tourist market on shore you can buy Burmese carpets, wood carvings, and other such things. Unfortunately, however, the goods are, on the whole, expensive, and you would be better to buy them in Bangkok or Chiang Mai.

Kanchanaburi

Kanchanaburi's calm, lush setting on the banks of the **Kwai River** belies its history, for it was here during World War II that thousands of prisoners of war died building the famous "Bridge over the River Kwai," as recounted in Pierre Boulle's novel and the film based on it.

You can still see the bridge, minus a couple of original sections that were bombed in 1945, and two trains cross it every day on their way to the town of Nam Tok (Waterfall), a pleasant hour's journey farther to the west.

When bargaining, you can generally expect to purchase the item at 50% to 75% of the first price quoted to you.

To get an idea of the horrors of building the bridge, visit the two cemeteries which contain over 8,000 graves of British, Dutch, Australian, Malaysian, Indian, New Zealand, Canadian, and Burmese prisoners and conscripts who died during the railway's construction, along with around 100,000 Asian civilians. The inscriptions on the gravestones are as simple and moving as tragic poems.

Those prepared to risk being run over by motorscooters and jostled by the crowds of locals should walk over the bridge to the other side. A safer way to view this tragic monument is from the long-tailed boats that hurtle up and down the river, stopping off at the cemetery and nearby caves.

Afterwards, you can drop in at the **JEATH Museum** on the river bank. Housed in a type of bamboo hut used in the prison camps, the exhibition documents Japanese atrocities in photographs, paintings, and relics. It also reveals the prisoners' ingenuity in surviving great hardships, as well as the sympathy and help which was secretly offered to the inmates by the local Thai population.

If you want to explore the countryside, adventurous businessmen have set up bases for tourists northwest of Kanchanaburi, in some of the most unspoilt scenery in the country. One hotel, next to the river, pampers its guests with air-conditioning and a swimming pool, while a couple of others, slightly more spartan, are built on bamboo rafts floating in the stream. Excursions to waterfalls, caves, and national parks can be arranged from these advance camps.

North of Bangkok

Ayutthaya

Undoubtedly the most enjoyable way to get to the ancient capital of Ayutthaya is by taking the luxurious cruiser up the Chao Phraya River that departs every day from outside the Oriental Hotel. On the way you will go past factories and

A gigantic statue in Ayutthaya is one of many relics restored in this city of archaeological wonders.

warehouses and, farther afield, rice fields and the beginnings of the countryside that stretches to Nakhon Sawan and the source of the Chao Phraya River hundreds of miles away.

Before exploring the great archaeological site itself, most tours stop at the nearby royal estate of **Bang Pa-In**. This collection of palaces set in gardens was built by King Chulalongkorn in the late 19th century. The names of palaces like "the Excellent and Shining Abode" and "the Sage's Lookout" are as delightful as the structures themselves. Nothing beats the splendid **Aisawan Thipha-at** (The Divine Seat of Personal Freedom), situated in the middle of the lake by which King Chulalongkorn (Rama V) composed odes as the sun went down.

Back on the highway, continue 20 km (12½ miles) south to the town of Ayutthaya, former capital of Thailand and home to one of its greatest civilizations. Here, where cattle still graze, you can climb the steps of ruined temples to look over the immensity of the ruined city, which was laid waste by the Burmese, who sacked the capital in 1767.

There are dozens of distinctive buildings, and you will be hard pressed to visit Ayutthaya in one day. For a tour of the ruins, it's best to start at **Wat Phra Si Sanphet**, on Si Sanphet Road, near the tourist car park (parking area). The temple was built in 1448 and once housed a 16-metre (52½-foot) Buddha image covered in gold and weighing 170 kilograms (375 pounds). In 1767 the Burmese set fire to it in order to melt off the gold, destroying both temple and image. What you can see are restored *chedis*, which hold the ashes of King Borom Trai Lokanat and his two sons.

At **Wat Phra Ram**, a graceful 14th-century building that is positioned amidst reflecting pools, there is a beautiful cloister lined with stone Buddha images, as well as several elephant gates, mythical *nagas,* and *garudas*. The temple was built in 1369 by King Ramesuan, on the site where his father was cremated.

For an overview of the art of the age of Ayutthaya, visit the **Chao Sam Phraya Museum**, stocked with the best statues discovered in the ruins. There are beautiful bronze Buddhas dating from the 13th and 14th centuries, as well as 17th- and 18th-century door panels with religious, traditional, or flower carvings, and a great hoard of 15th-century gold jewellery.

Next, visit **Wat Mahathat**, built in 1384 by King Ramesuan. Once, it con-

With 375 temples and 29 fortresses to see, Ayutthaya is best explored with a cyclo-driver.

tained treasures of precious stones, gold, and crystal, and a relic of the Lord Buddha in a gold casket, which is now housed in the National Museum (see page 30).

Wat Rachaburan, next to Wat Mahathat, was built in the 15th century around the tombs of Prince Ay and Prince Yi, brothers who slew each other in a tragic battle on elephant-back. Rare frescoes remain in the crypt, but any portable antiquities were stolen years ago.

Finish off with a visit to the **Elephant Kraal**, a few miles from town, where hunters used to drive large herds (up to 200 animals) of wild elephants into the stockade. Once captured they were put into the king's service, either as fighters or, if they were the rare white type, as symbols of power. The last capture was in 1903 during the reign of King Chulalongkorn.

Southeast of Bangkok

Ancient City

If your time is limited, there is no need to go to Sukhothai (see page 51) and Ayutthaya to see the ancient capitals. A far-sighted temple buff made the trip unnecessary by building models of them in what is said to be the largest outdoor museum in the world, 33 km (20 miles) southeast of Bangkok. Laid out as a map of Thailand and covering roughly 81 hectares (200

Founding a Dynasty

According to legend, Ayutthaya was founded by the illegitimate son of a princess, who was discovered to be pregnant after eating an aubergine on which a gardener had relieved himself! U-Thong, or Prince of the Golden Crib, as the son was named, became the first of 33 ruling kings, while the kingdom became the largest and most beautiful in the East and the principal kingdom in Siam for over four centuries.

acres), Ancient City re-cre-
ates the country's greatest
buildings in either full-sized
or slightly reduced scale.
The parks also boast exotic
birds, monkeys, and ele-
phants, which keep the children happy. Travel agents
run half-day outings to Ancient City, or there are daily
buses from Bangkok.

Crocodile Farm

Another 5 km (3 miles) along
the road from Ancient City is
the Crocodile Farm at Samut
Prakarn. This huge enclosure
is billed as the world's largest
establishment of its kind,
with the total "croc" popula-

*Thailand's most beloved
animal is as popular
as ever, but, sadly, its
numbers are dwindling.*

tion put at almost 30,000. The farm two purposes: it preserves
endangered species at the same time as entertaining and edu-
cating the public. The travel agencies in Bangkok run half-day
tours, or you can take a bus there yourself.

Northeast of Bangkok

Khao Yai

The vast national park at Khao Yai rises from the Korat plat-
eau, baked dry in summer and lush with greenery and flowers following the rains. Khao Yai means "big mountain," and
the resort, which is located three hours' drive from Bangkok,
is both the oldest and one of the best in the kingdom.

Tourists step back in time during an outing at the Ancient City. This Khmer-style shrine is a reminder of a bygone era.

The park covers 2,100 square km (837 square miles), and within its boundaries are elephants and over 100 other species, including Asian wild dog, clouded leopard, and black bear, all still running wild. Keep an eye out for some of Thailand's most significant bird concentrations, among which are some of the largest groups of hornbills in Southeast Asia, moustached barbets, orange-breasted and red-headed trogons, and great slaty woodpeckers.

Although wildlife sightings are neither consistently common nor, for that matter, guaranteed, pleasant walks to giant waterfalls help to occupy any spare time, and nighttime safaris employ spotlights to pick out deer, tropical birds, and, if you're lucky, tigers and bears.

Before being declared a national park in 1959, Khao Yai was known as a sanctuary not just for animals, but also as a popular hiding place for outlaws. This, of course, is no longer the case, and now the park offers hotels, a restaurant, and an 18-hole golf course.

Phimai

Phimai, some 68 km (42 miles) northeast, is known for its ancient religious compound at the end of the long, dusty main street.

Built during King Jayavarman VI's reign in the 12th century, and situated just a short distance from the Cambodian border, Phimai was probably designed by Khmer architects, for it is similar in style to the magnificent Angkor Wat (see page 80). Four gates dominate the ruins, the largest preceded by a *naga* bridge guarded by lions. Adorning the elegant arcades of the cloisters are intricate engravings of flowers, elephants, and monkeys.

Inside the inner courtyard stand two small *stupas* (Prang Hin Daeng and Prang Phromathat), and in the centre there is an ornate dome with doors and a lintel, intricately carved with scenes related to Mahayana Buddhism.

Outside in the gardens there is an open-air museum, which contains a collection of ancient friezes, statues, and stone lintels of Buddha, gods, and monkeys. These were gathered all over northeast Thailand prior to being amassed here.

A pleasant way to round off the trip is to visit the larger-than-life (or at least taller than a house) **banyan tree**, which stands 2 km (1 mile) farther down the road and is said to be the biggest in the world. Delicious Isaan food is served in its shade, but only in the dry season. During the wet season, the nearby reservoir floods the picnic ground. If spirits live in trees—as many Thais believe—then this prodigious banyan is surely thronged with ghosts.

PATTAYA

Visitors rarely come to Pattaya for palm-fringed beaches and tropical seas, for this infamous resort, sited 147 km (91 miles) southeast of Bangkok, lost its original attractions to pollution many years ago. What Pattaya does have—and in abundance—is fun, along with a nightlife that eclipses even Bangkok's.

Although King Taksin once set up camp in the vicinity 200 years ago, he failed to give the seashore a second thought. In the ensuing years, little of consequence happened to the village until 1961, when the first American servicemen arrived for what was soon described as "R & R"—rest and recreation. The Thais eventually realized Pattaya's commercial possibilities, and the area fast became a thriving international resort.

Today, there are over 20,000 hotel rooms or bungalows here officially considered to meet with international standards of comfort. Hundreds more, suitable for budget travellers, are found near the seafront strip, surrounded by bars and clubs.

Most hotels have swimming pools, since these days the sea around Pattaya is not recommended. Indeed, if swimming is what you are after, take a boat trip to the outlying coral islands. Alternatively, catch a *baht* bus (river bus) to the beach at Jomtien, a 15-minute trip south, where clean sand stretches for several miles, with only a few glistening new condominiums.

Adventurous visitors to Pattaya might consider trying out parasailing, while others may prefer a day's deep-sea fishing, relishing the opportunity to try catching delicious snapper and sizeable marlin. Countless excursion boats take tourists to islands in the surrounding area for swimming and snorkelling in clear blue seas.

At **Ko Larn**, about 45 minutes from Pattaya in a converted trawler or half the time in a speedboat, you can explore the underwater world in a glass-bottomed boat, gazing at vivid tropical fish and coral—albeit now sadly depleted compared with a few years ago. Some scuba expeditions begin here with a workout, before going on to a couple of wrecks which lie farther south, near Sattahip.

Land tours are just as easy to arrange, and you might visit **Nong Nooch**, an exotic village 15 km (9 miles) to the east, for daily displays of folk dances, martial arts, and (the controversial) cock fighting, as well as a vast acreage of exotic palms, orchids, and cacti. If that's not your scene, try **Mini Siam**, a miniature town which contains more than 100 historic towns on a scale of 1:25, or there is always the **Elephant Kraal**, where elephants show off their strength, skill, and obedience. Keen equestrians should head for **Reo Park Ranch**, 30 minutes from Pattaya, for a gallop on thoroughbreds.

When you return, there are plenty of culinary delights as well, since the restaurants in Pattaya serve first-rate seafood—shrimp, clams, crab, lobster, oyster, prawns, and a variety of others. What's more, you don't have to be in luxury hotels to feast on such delights; simple waterfront restaurants provide dishes that are just as tasty, but at a fraction of the five-star price. Those who prefer French fries and *bratwurst* shouldn't worry either—you'll be just as well catered for as everyone else.

Pattaya's nightlife, too, has something to satisfy almost all tastes, from big musical productions and the world-famous transvestite shows, to discotheques, nightclubs, beer bars—and all those other establishments that have earned this area its reputation as the international entertainment resort of Thailand.

Hua Hin

You can easily bypass Pattaya and opt for quieter charms at Hua Hin, 220 km (136½ miles) southwest of Bangkok on the opposite shore of the Gulf of Thailand, once favoured by the royal family. The odd condominium has now blotted out some of its royal views, and its long, sweeping beaches are no longer as pleasant as they once were for swimming. They do however make fine strolling ground, and with its lazy deckchairs, pony riding, and golf courses, Hua Hin is far removed from Pattaya.

CENTRAL THAILAND

The most striking thing about the central region is its sheer abundance, for this vast, fertile plain that starts at Bangkok's busy outskirts is the country's rice bowl, home to one-third of the population, and site of one of the biggest rice crops in the world. Centuries ago, this agricultural heartland also played host to some of the kingdom's greatest civilizations, amongst them those of Si Satchanalai, Sukhothai, and Lop Buri, ancient cities that remain as enchanting in ruins as they must have been in their heyday.

Major towns in the area are easily visited from Bangkok, and make good stop-off points en route to the northern region.

Pattaya beaches—once the perfect place to relax in the sun and enjoy the ocean—have been tainted by pollution.

☞ Lop Buri

Lop Buri's dominant features are the superb stone temples built by the Khmers. These can be seen even from the railway station, as can the French-style architecture and several hundred monkeys which have become this town's other lasting claim to fame.

Originally one of the capitals of the Khmer people, Lop Buri flourished under Thai rule in the 17th century. King Narai chose the town as an alternative capital, in case some unforeseen fate befell Ayutthaya. His caution did not go without justification, as Ayutthaya was sacked by the Burmese the following century.

Begin your tour at the **Phra Narai Rajanivet Palace**. This magnificent building was constructed with the aid of

Monkeys find a watermelon feast in Lop Buri.

French architects in the mid-17th century, and took longer than 12 years to complete. Inside is the National Museum, housing exquisite examples of Khmer art. The palace also incorporates the old treasure houses, a banquet hall, an audience hall for high-ranking foreign visitors, and the stables where the king kept his elephants and horses.

After the palace, pay a visit to **Vichayen House**, originally the residence of the Chevalier de Chaumont, the first French ambassador to Thailand. Later it was the residence of Constantine Phaulkon (see page 16).

Near Vichayen House, **Wat Phra Si Ratana Mahathat** is a fine example of 12th-century Khmer-style architecture, with *chedis* built in Sukhothai style.

Lop Buri's famous monkeys can be found by the railway in the Kala Shrine, and in nearby Phra Prang Sam Yod, a magnificent 13th-century temple with three distinctive *prangs* from which they like to hang, begging food and fruit from visitors. Make sure you keep firm hold of your camera and other valuables, as monkeys clutching stolen goods are far from an uncommon sight.

Sukhothai

Sukhothai, the most striking of Thailand's various spectacular ruined cities, lies 427 km (265 miles) north of Bangkok, surrounded by rice fields and distant hills. Built in the late 13th and early 14th centuries under the legendary King Ramkamhaeng, it flourished for almost 150 years until vanquished by Ayutthaya, and its people fled. Until around 40 years ago, the ancient capital was hidden by jungle, the outlines of the classical towers camouflaged by a heavy green undergrowth. The situation now is better, for in a huge renovation programme implemented by UNESCO and Thailand's government, some 200 moats, kilns, images, and temples have been restored to the glory of earlier days. These lie within the boundaries of the historical park, 13 km (8 miles) west of the new town of Sukhothai, and are reached easily by *songthaew*, reconditioned jeeps with seats in the back, which carry as many passengers as can be squeezed in.

For a delightful insight into the past and a glimpse of some of the finest sculptures, start at the **National Museum**, near to the Kamphang Hek Gate. This houses a splendid 14th-century example of the Walking Buddha, the image that, according to archaeologists, is the finest of all Thai Buddhas. A replica of King Ramkamhaeng's famous inscription is also on show. This is the earliest example of Thai script and an oft-repeated quotation from Thai literature: "In the water there are fish, in the fields there is rice . . . Those who choose to laugh, laugh, those who choose to cry, cry."

A short walk past the moat brings you to **Wat Mahathat**, temple of the Great Relic. This is the biggest and finest temple in Sukhothai, dating from the 14th century and housing rows of the standing Buddha images known as Phra Attharot.

Continue by visiting beautiful **Wat Sra Si** (Temple of the Splendid Pond), with its graceful image of the walking Buddha and slender *chedi* shaped like a bell, and **Wat Trapang Ngoen**, situated around a large lake which floods occasionally during the rainy season.

Carry on to the west outside the walled city and you reach **Wat Sri Chum**, with its massive seated Buddha measuring 11½ metres (37 feet) from knee to knee, and each finger the size of a man. The sanctuary walls are 3-metres (10-feet) thick and contain a secret passage off to the left just inside the entrance. This was used by the king, though for what purpose is not clear.

The temple of **Wat Saphan Hin**, 2 km (1 mile) west of the city, is known as the Temple of the Stone Bridge, after the slate pathway leading up the hill. It is a long haul to the summit, on which stands a Buddha statue more than 12 metres (40 feet) tall. However—and especially in the cool of the late afternoon—it is a trip that is well worth the effort.

The best time of year to visit Sukhothai is on the full moon of the 12th lunar month (mid-November), when Thailand's most beautiful and serene festival, known as *Loi Krathong*, is celebrated. It is believed to have started some 700 years ago, after one of the king's concubines fashioned a lantern from carved fruit and sent it floating down the river

The ruins at Sukhothai: legend says the city was founded by a freedom fighter in 1238.

bearing a lighted candle. Now, thousands of people gather by the lake to launch boats made of banana leaves and to marvel at colourful processions of the local women and a tremendous display of fireworks.

Si Satchanalai

If you still have a craving for more temples, you may like to consider taking an afternoon's excursion to the city of Satchanalai, 55 km (34 miles) to the north of Sukhothai.

This is the sister city of Sukhothai, but is wilder and less visited by tourists, with ramshackle temples and an atmospheric air of faded grandeur. At the top of a steep flight of

Harvesting the Rice

In Thailand's endless green paddies, peasant women in lampshade hats are as common a sight as water buffalo.

For much of the year, up to 70 percent of the population works the fields, tilling the soil or sowing the rice, toiling from dawn to nightfall, then taking the water buffalo home, cooking, and sleeping.

This is an endless cycle, dictated by the rains and the sun; those involved go on oblivious to events in the outside world. When the harvest is over, planting begins anew in time for the next rains; so it has been for centuries.

Gilded Buddhas at the Wat Mahathat are believed to have the power to cure diseases.

steps is the ruined **Wat Khao Suwan Khiri**, which is worth the climb for the views alone.

Hire a bicycle from outside the historical park and explore what many regard as the city's most impressive temple, **Wat Chang Lom** (which translates literally as "Elephant Temple"). The *chedi* is surrounded by 39 standing elephants and a stairway which represents a ladder to heaven. Real elephants can usually be found in front of the temple, and it is often possible to get rides around the park—although they are not cheap.

In nearby Ban Khao Noi, a village 4 km (2½ miles) to the north, archaeologists have discovered kilns that might prove that the Thais began producing pottery 400 years earlier than the Chinese.

Phitsanulok

A wide river cuts right through the heart of Phitsanulok, about 370 km (229 miles) to the north of Bangkok, and separates the old part of town into two. Although the broad banks of the River Nan can make a pleasant spot to rest, the real attraction is **Wat Mahathat**.

Believers have been coming here for centuries, praying in front of the renowned golden Chinarat Buddha, famous for its curative powers. The temple, with lovely mother-of-pearl doors from King Boromkot, was built in 1357, and its shrine is so popular that Thai tourists swarm here every day. To meet this demand, a variety of shops in the complex stock pendants, relics, and other souvenirs.

Apart from Wat Mahathat, there are few reminders of the town's great history. A giant fire destroyed most of the old town several years ago, and now it is best known for comfortable hotels and as a base for Sukhothai excursions.

NORTHERN THAILAND

Stretching up to the Myanmar (Burma) and Laos borders and following the line of the great Mekong River, northern Thailand incorporates some of the most beautiful scenery in the country. This region was once divided into small principalities which were isolated by the rugged terrain and accessible only by elephant. Even today people speak their own dialect—influenced by Burmese and Lhao—and retain their own culinary specialities. Getting there for today's visitor, however, is a simpler process than before, with regular planes and trains leaving from Bangkok. In five days, it is easily possible to explore the area around Chiang Mai and Chiang Rai—and even to take a trek among the northern hill tribes.

Chiang Mai

Chiang Mai, the capital of the north, rises from the banks of the Ping River, bedecked with flowers and orchid blossoms in the spring. Formerly no more than a hillside Shangri-la, the town has grown rapidly to become both a tourist mecca and a major city in its own right— with the traffic and pollution to match. Several thousand luxury rooms and cheap and cheerful guesthouses are available, as well as European-style bars and restaurants. Tour operators offer countless trips to colourful handicraft villages, hillside temples, and mountain tribes.

After the heat of Bangkok, the more temperate climate of Chiang Mai comes as a relief. The cooler weather is immediately evident (pack a sweater if you're here between October and January), and so too is the abundance of fruit, vegetables, and flowers, which can be seen at almost any time of year.

Chiang Mai, meaning "new town," was founded by King Mengrai the Great at the end of the 13th century (see page 13). According to one legend, the city wall—parts of which can still be seen—was built by 90,000 men, working in shifts round-the-clock. Mengrai also built various temples and fine buildings, some of which remain and can be explored on foot or by hiring a bicycle or motorbike. Don't forget to go to the handicraft centres nearby for silk, painted umbrellas, and lacquerware.

Thai Airways International flies to Chiang Mai in less than an hour from Bangkok, while air-conditioned express buses make the run in about 9 hours, and overnight express trains in 12 to 14 hours.

Inside the City

Start your tour of this delightful city at **Wat Chiang Man**, within the old city walls. Built in the 13th century under

King Mengrai, it contains two well-known religious statues —the Crystal and Marble Buddhas, protected behind a railing, bars, and glass—which were ancient long before this monastery had been conceived. Sculpted elephants surround a *chedi* at the rear of this temple.

Walk south for 15 minutes and you reach the huge, ruined *chedi* of **Wat Chedi Luang**. Built by King Saen Muang Ma in the 15th century, it was subsequently damaged during an earthquake over 400 years ago. In the temple grounds stands a gigantic gum tree shrouded in silk which, it is said, will continue to grow for as long as the city prospers. Beneath the tree, locals leave wooden elephants and phallic objects as offerings to the guardian spirit of the city.

Red-shingled temple rooftops are typical in Chiang Mai.

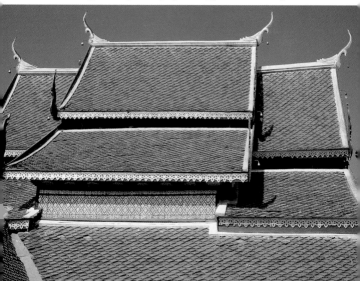

Continue west to find **Wat Phra Singh**, which contains a magnificent Buddha. According to legend, the image was on its way to the king when the chariot carrying it broke down in front of the temple. Believing this to be a signal that the image wished to go no farther, the people installed it without question, and there it has remained ever since, along with a beautiful library and several fine carvings and sculptures.

The best time of day to visit **Wat Suan Dok** (The Flower Garden Temple), which is off Cherng Doy Road on the city outskirts, is at sunset, when the *chedi* is bathed in soft, golden rays. The ashes of the kings of Lanna are housed within the temple, which is said also to hold an important relic of the Buddha, brought here by elephant.

A final temple not to miss is **Wat Chet Yot**, known as the Seven Peaks, due to its seven *chedis*. Local guides say it was inspired by a great Mahabodi Indian temple in 1455, during the reign of King Tilokaraja.

For visitors who want other entertainment, Chiang Mai has plenty to offer. Drop in at the **Folk Art Museum**, in a charming old northern-style house, which sells some of the finest northern wood carvings and antiques; or explore markets like **Somphet** (Moonmuang Road), or busy **Warorot** (Wichyanon Road), where you can try delicious local delicacies, including *khao soi* (a spicy noodle dish) and spicy *naem* sausages. Finally, in the evening, don't miss the **Night Market** on Chang Klan Road, which offers dazzling northern handicrafts. You'll be overwhelmed by the sheer variety, which is probably greater here than at any other market in Thailand. If all that shopping makes you hungry, there are plenty of restaurants to try nearby.

Outside the City

Explore the following as part of either a half-day tour or a more extended itinerary.

Wat Suan Dok—the Flower Garden—is the keeper of the ashes of the kings of Lanna.

Elephant lovers will want to make it to the **elephant camp** at Mae Taem, 63 km (39 miles) north from Chiang Mai, where you can still see the vast creatures learning the arts of timber lifting and bathing. Years ago, elephants were a common sight throughout the north, for they were used both for transport across inhospitable terrain and for dragging logs down to the river, where they could be floated downstream.

These days, elephants are the objects of more theatrical attention, with morning shows and river washing staged for visitors. You can actually have a ride on one of the giants of the jungle, and then afterwards take a raft trip through the lush countryside, alive with colourful birds.

Wooden statues, huge clay pots, and gaily coloured paper umbrellas bedeck the road to the village of **San Kamphaeng**, which lies 13 km (8 miles) east of Chiang Mai and is known as the handicrafts centre of northern Thailand. In the factories and warehouses, you can watch the locals as they weave silk from cocoons or make lacquerware or painted umbrellas, a process that has changed little over the years. Afterwards, stock up on the best and brightest gifts in the kingdom. Purchases can be shipped home, and credit cards are widely accepted.

To visit Chiang Mai's most famous temple—and for stunning views of the surrounding region—travel the 25-minute bus ride to **Wat Phrathat Doi Suthep**, which overlooks town from atop a hill. From the car park (parking lot), it's a 300-step hike (or a comfortable funicular ride) to the central gold *chedi* at the top, with its royal bronze parasols at each corner. The cloister is lined with many Buddha statues of artistic importance.

Orchid Mania

Some of Thailand's remote areas are happy breeding grounds for over 1,000 different varieties of orchid, ranging from the famous *Pa-phiopedium ascocenda* to the elegant "Miss Udorn Sunshine." The best place to see them is at the orchid farms in the area around Chiang Mai, although you only need to look in markets throughout the country to see and appreciate the kingdom's favourite flower.

Continue another 4 km (2½ miles) past the temple to reach the **Winter Palace** (Phu Ping Palace), where the Thai king and queen often spend some of the winter. If the royal family is not in residence, at weekends and holidays the grounds are opened to the public in a blaze of lavish floral displays.

One final attraction in the vicinity is the small Hmong or Meo village called **Doi Pui**. Since it is the most accessible of all Thailand's hill-tribe villages, you are unlikely to find much authenticity. Still, if you don't have enough time to go trekking, the village does give an idea of the hill tribes' way of life, and also includes a visit to the opium museum. Crowds of children sell colourful costumes, tassled bags, and primitive handicrafts.

Trekking into the Hills

To see the tribes in a more authentic environment, go along with an organized trek into the hills. You will probably have to walk considerable distances and sleep on less than luxurious floors, but with a guide's aid, you can still locate numerous Karen tribes, who believe in the spirits of the winds and the rains, or the Lahu people, the men in silver buckles and black turbans and women in calf-length tunics with yellow or white embroidery.

At Wat Phrathat Doi Suthep a woman engages in the daily religious ritual of burning incense.

Known as the *chao doi*, the hill tribes are nomadic peoples who have migrated from Tibet and southern China along various routes into Burma, Thailand, and Laos. In all, there are some

500,000 of them, divided into six tribes: the Karen, Meo, Akha, Yao, Lisu, and Lahu, each with its own distinct dress, language, and culture.

Generally, they are highland dwellers who opt to live above 1,000 metres (3,280 feet). They earn a living from foraging, slash-and-burn agriculture, and raising domestic livestock such as chickens and black pigs; all inter-tribal trade is done by barter. Traditionally, the *chao doi* have also shared a common mythology. They believe that they live on top of a dragon and that they have to keep the peace to ensure that it does not move.

The Karen: of all the tribes, the Karen or Yang Karing are the most numerous, their population standing at approximately 265,000. Concentrated on the whole in the mountainous area along the western border with Burma, they are probably the oldest tribe, having been in Thailand for over 250 years.

The Meo: the next largest group is the Meo (Hmong), who are found mainly around Chiang Mai, Chiang Rai, and Mae Hong Son. One of the proudest of the tribal people, they worship the spirit of the sky, which they believe created the world and their way of life.

The Akha: thought to number roughly 33,000, the Akha came from Yunnan in southern China and live mainly in extended family units, which are a hallmark of traditional Akha life. Worshipping the sun and moon, the Akhas also fear the spirits in the swamps and termite mounds.

The Yao: the Yao are found mainly in the surroundings of Chiang Rai, o, and Nan, and can often be identified by their teeth capped with gold—a popular sign of wealth—their ankle-length tunics, and thick, purple sashes around the neck. The Yao have traditionally cultivated opium and believe in polygamous marriages and extended families.

The Lisu: spread throughout nine northern provinces, the Lisu is the most widely dispersed hill tribe. In total there are

Treks to villages, such as the Akha, are great ways to learn about these fascinating cultures first-hand.

around 24,000 of them, divided into the black Lisu and Hua Lisu. They only started to migrate roughly 60 years ago, coming from southern China.

The Lahu: of Tibetan origin, the Lahu are poorer than other tribes and number somewhere in the region of 55,000. They are mainly concentrated north of Chiang Rai and in the Fang area; you can often distinguish the men by their silver buckles and black turbans, and the women by calf-length tunics with embroidery.

Travel agencies in Chiang Mai operate excursions ranging from one-day trips to more rewarding three- and four-day expeditions. Don't expect too much originality, though—villagers may ask for payment for posing for photos, and while some are friendly and seem to be pleased that their colourful bejewelled costumes and simple huts are a centre of attention, others have discarded just about every trace of their traditions, opting instead for jeans, T-shirts, and Pepsi-Cola.

It's always worth dropping in to the tourist office to check which are the reliable trekking companies, as they can change from month to month. Be sure to use a guide who can speak English and, if at all possible, the tribal tongue as well, since this will greatly add to the success of the trip.

Lamphun

Although legend has it that the most beautiful women in Thailand are from Lamphun, this is not the only reason for coming to this peaceful, ancient town, which can be found 30 km (18½ miles) south of Chiang Mai.

A large monastery in the town centre called **Wat Phrathat Haripunchai** is a busy educational and meditational institution. The huge, gold *chedi* in the middle of the monastery was begun over one thousand years ago, and the workmen who erected it constructed their own simpler version outside the compound; it is now a ruin. Close by and built in modern style is the National Museum, which has a collection of sculptures found in the Lamphun district, dating from the 10th to 12th centuries.

You can take a pedicab from the centre of Lamphun to **Wat Chama Devi** (or Kukut), a temple that owes its existence to Princess Chama Devi, who is said to have founded it when she ruled the Mon kingdom of Lamphun well over a thousand years ago. Of the original elements, the most memorable is a *chedi* rising in five tiers with 60 standing Buddha images in stucco around the sides.

Look out for the *lamyai* orchards that have helped make this region famous throughout Thailand. This delicious fruit, known as longan in English, resembles a lychee.

Lampang

Don't be surprised if you see a horse and carriage slowly trundling down the main road of this beautiful old town, 100 km (62 miles) southeast of Chiang Mai—this is Lampang's main form of transport, and the best way to explore.

There are three temples here that deserve special mention. **Wat Phra Fang** boasts a tall, white *chedi* with seven small shrines around the base. **Wat Phra Kaew Don Toa** reveals Burmese influence and has outstanding carvings. **Wat Phrathat Lampang Luang**, situated 18 km (11 miles) from Lampang near the town of Ko Kha, is worth a visit for its museum and fine Buddha images.

Chiang Rai

The most exciting way of arriving in Chiang Rai, a city 180 km (111½ miles) to the north of Chiang Mai, is not by the route through the hills, nor by the 45-minute flight, but by the least comfortable option of the river boat from the town of Tha Ton. This is a trip for the adventurous—the boats are both small and narrow, with no toilets, while the engine is as loud (but not as powerful) as an aeroplane. Nonetheless, it is worth the effort, for the views on the four-hour journey are spectacular.

Chiang Rai is mainly of use as a base from which to visit regional attractions, and you'll need to travel a short way out of this undistinguished town in order to see them. King Mengrai founded Chiang Rai in the 13th century, by chance so it is said. According to legend, his elephant ran off and took him to a spot on the Mae Kok River, where the scenery and military potential of the place inspired him to build a town. In recent years, town planners have unfortunately seen fit to fill it up with car showrooms and ugly concrete buildings.

Still, there are at least two temples worth a visit. At **Wat Phra Kaeo**, you can see a former home of the Emerald Buddha (see page 27), the country's most famous image. At the Burmese-style **Wat Doi Chom Thong**, you have the bonus of views of the river below and a glimpse of the town's old section.

Travel agencies in Chiang Rai operate excursions to the famous, hillside temple of **Doi Tung**, perched some 1,800 metres (5,904 feet) up the mountain. On the way there you will pass the Queen Mother's summer residence and a royal-sponsored agricultural project designed to help the hill tribes integrate into contemporary life. The tribespeople are encouraged to grow strawberries, cucumbers, and cabbages in lieu of opium, and in return receive government schools, new roads, and income from tourists who come here to purchase their wares.

Smaller tribal villages can also still be found in the mountains north of Chiang Rai and the area around Mae Chan. Be warned, however: pigs, water buffalo, and dogs may still wander picturesquely among the stilt houses, but modern life has not passed by unnoticed, and the children will ask for coins or, increasingly, notes. Even among the Yao villages of adobe huts with thatched roofs, many elders have learned a few English words. The women, in red collared jackets and blue turbans, are usually more interested in selling handicrafts than telling of the Yao's origins in southern China more than two hundred years ago.

Mae Sai and Chiang Saen

You can't go farther north in Thailand than Mae Sai; beyond is the footbridge across the Sai River into Burma. This charming little backwater with a sprinkling of markets and guesthouses is a good lunchtime spot on the way to the Golden Triangle.

Get there between 6:00 A.M. and 6:00 P.M. and you'll see authorized travellers from Burma crossing the border into Thailand to sell products which they bring in by hand: cheroots, packaged prunes, ivory carvings, lacquer boxes, oranges, and, more discreetly, items such as gems and contraband cigarettes.

In the market, take your pick from the wonderful Burmese puppets and tapestries known as *kalaga*, or pay your Bt10 to photograph children dressed in hill-tribe costume. If you're in luck, you may go to the end of the bridge to purchase exotic Burmese vegetables or other innocuous local products.

From Mae Sai, tours usually continue the 12 km (7½ miles) to the infamous Golden Triangle, which forms a three-way border between Burma, Laos, and Thailand. This spot, like many others, once saw huge quantities of opium being sent across the border, destined for heroin traders in Paris and New York.

Now, the figure is dropping, as a result of government encouragement to diversify into less sinister crops. Poppies won't be seen here, since discretion confines cultivation to the less accessible valleys, as well as to those vast areas in

A view from the treetops into the tribal village in Chiang Rai.

Burma which are controlled by the so-called "opium armies" and the famous prince of poppies, Khun Sa.

A short drive west from Ban Sop Ruak will bring you to the friendly little town of **Chiang Saen,** set in a marvellous location on the gentle banks of the mighty Mekong River.

Despite its dilapidated feel, this town boasts a remarkably grand history. From the 10th to 13th centuries it was the seat of power for one of the earliest northern principalities—traces of this glorious past are scattered through what has since become a sleepy market town. You can easily spend an afternoon exploring a moated city wall, Wat Phra That Chom Kitti—reputed to house part of Lord Buddha's forehead—the ruins of several other temples, and a museum showing Stone Age utensils and statues from Chiang Saen's golden era. Visitors who have more time for leisurely travelling may also be rewarded with beautiful sunsets over the great Mekong River, and marvellous views of Laos, just a stone's throw away.

Mae Hong Son

December and January are the prime months to visit the town of Mae Hong Son, which lies squeezed between mountains 270 km (167½ miles) northwest of Chiang Mai and is reached by a hair-raising but staggeringly beautiful eight-hour road trip or a less bumpy 30-minute flight. At this time of year, the sky is at its bluest, the winter flowers blossom, and the air is lush and cool. It doesn't really matter what month you come, however, for this city offers no shortage of attractions.

Until 1831, when an expedition was sent there by the king of Chiang Mai in search of the rare white elephant, Mae Hong Son's history was as misty as its valleys. The expedition was so successful, however, that a small settlement was founded, and by 1874 Mae Hong Son was a provincial capital.

Akha girls in traditional costume pose for photographs on the bridge to Burma at Mae Sai.

Although you're unlikely to see wild elephants, what you will come across are Burmese-style temples standing on the banks of the Jongkhum Lake, framed against the distant hills. Most people like exploring the market at dawn—when the hill-tribe people in traditional dress can sometimes be seen buying vegetables—before going on any of the variety of tours. Guides arrange elephant riding and river rafting, or will drive you to tribal villages at the Burmese border.

The sight of Padang's **"long-necked people,"** with necks as long as 30 centimetres (12 inches), will not be to everyone's taste. Legend has it that the tribe's ancestors were a female dragon and the wind god, and it was in imitation of the image of the dragon that the women took up the unusual "long-neck" tradition. Inevitably, the reality now is that this ungainly appearance helps attract tourists.

In the area surrounding Mae Hong Son you have the chance to explore caves and waterfalls or merely breathe in the fresh air of the mountains (either jeeps or motorbikes can be hired). Keen drivers and bus passengers can return to Chiang Mai on a circular route that goes via Mae Sariang and Hot, so that towns visited previously are not repeated. Visitors who can't face another tortuous and winding eight-hour trip have the option of taking the plane.

SOUTHERN THAILAND

Southern Thailand, stretching thinly down to Malaysia, gives you a choice of seas. The considerably longer eastern coast is on the Gulf of Thailand, while the west is washed by the Indian Ocean. On either side, though, you'll find sensational beaches, while the land between— rice fields and coconut and rubber plantations—is as scenic as it is fertile. Planes fly to Phuket and Ko Samui from Bangkok; otherwise, there are trains and buses and the opportunity to explore several of the small, picturesque fishing villages along the way.

Stilt houses are a common sight along the banks of the Mekong River.

Phuket

The island of Phuket (pronounced poo-ket) is Thailand's top beach destination, with some of the most beautiful beaches and luxurious hotels in the land, in addition to sailing, snorkeling, and nightlife.

Covering around 810 square km (313 square miles) and made up of a mountainous interior, Phuket offers over a dozen white-sand beaches, as well as national parks, inland plantations, and waterfalls.

It attracts over one million tourists every year—almost six times the island's total population—most of whom arrive by plane (55 minutes from Bangkok), although tourist coaches also do the journey, in just over 14 hours, crossing the causeway from the mainland.

Although Phuket has been transformed by the invasion of tourists, and new hotels are almost as abundant as water buffalo, you are nonetheless spoilt with some of the most beautiful scenery and clearest seas in the region.

Even historians might find something to interest them in Phuket. From the airport, the highway south goes through a dusty village called **Thalang**, the site of the island's ancient

Korrekt Spelling

Thai signmakers often transliterate names into English, but with glorious inconsistency. Sometimes you see Petchburi, or often Petburi, Phetchburi, or Phetburi. In the same way, the island of Phuket (pronounced poo-ket) can be spelt with rather unfortunate connotations. This underlines the difficulty of trying to speak Thai—a language with 48 vowels and 44 consonants, and which is fiendishly tonal: the word ma means "horse," "dog" or "to come," depending on how it is pronounced.

capital. Burmese invaders besieged, pillaged, and destroyed Thalang in 1809. In an earlier and more positive chapter of history, the city managed to withstand a siege by the Burmese which went on for longer than a month. This battle, in 1786, led to both Lady Muk and her sister Lady Chan being regarded as heroines for taking command of the town's defence following the death of Lady Muk's husband, the governor. Statues of these short-haired women warriors stand in a traffic circle on the road.

The new capital, also called Phuket or Phuket Town, is not so much a sight in its own right as more of a departure and arrival point. A couple of streets of traditional two-storey Sino-Portuguese houses have been preserved, and a host of shopping centres, cafés, and excellent seafood restaurants can be found. Souvenir shops still sell coral, wonderful seashells, and locally cultivated—as well as counterfeited—pearls.

Most visitors, however, find it hard to tear themselves away from the sun and sea. Watersports of all kinds are offered, from waterskiing to paragliding, and windsurfers, catamarans, and yachts can be hired. Fresh seafood makes for memorable meals, and everyone at some stage treats themselves to the famous Phuket lobster, which is best eaten grilled and with a dash of lime.

Beaches and Islands

The best beaches are on the west coast of the island, where fine, white sand slopes slowly into the Andaman Sea (Indian Ocean). **Patong Beach**, 15 km (9 miles) west of Phuket Town by paved road, is the island's most beautiful and most developed, packed with bungalows, hotels, restaurants, bars, pubs, and discotheques.

The marvellous beaches of **Kata** and **Karon** are less developed, though rapid building has provided an abundance of

Harvestors in the luscious fruit fields of southern Thailand.

tasteful family resorts offering every comfort. More secluded is **Pansea**, home to the Amanpuri and Pansea hotels, two of the quietest and most exclusive addresses on the island. A bit farther south at Nai Harn you will find a few more of Phuket's beach bungalows, squeezed in between two rocky headlands.

It is possible to hire a jeep to tour the island, but be warned that some roads are steep and accidents are not uncommon. The most dramatic viewing point is the **Laem Promthep** promontory, which is 19 km (12 miles) southwest of Phuket Town.

The sea views from Phuket are dotted with 30 or so uninhabited islands, to which owners of long-tailed boats operate excursions from some beaches for picnics and/or snorkelling. Local experts say the grounds for scuba diving are first rate, with plenty of coral and brilliantly hued fish. Even better are the Similan Islands, which have national marine park status. Deep-sea expeditions can be arranged to catch mackerel, barracuda, and sailfish.

Excursions from Phuket

Phuket travel agencies offer a variety of day-long excursions. Anyone who knows the James Bond film *The Man with the Golden Gun* will not want to miss visiting **Phangnga**, where the bay contains the superb, mushroom-shaped rock formations featured in the film, and which still lure holidaymakers with their exotic appeal. Long-tailed boats skim through the mangrove into a dreamscape of mad mountain-tops, and at two points of the journey sail through tunnels beneath limestone islands worn by the tides.

On the way they will stop at **Panyi** island, where the Muslim fishing people have built a village on stilts above the sea and now enjoy the attention of thousands of tourists, who buy their woodwork and fresh fish.

The real highlight, though, is **Ko Tapu** (meaning literally "nail island"), which was formed thousands of years ago as a result of an earthquake. The island rises straight up out of the water to a height of 200 metres (656 feet).

Adventurers can escape the crowds by hiring boats to more distant, uninhabited islands—just make sure that before leaving you agree on the price and the number of islands that you will be visiting.

A separate excursion is offered to the beautiful **Phi Phi islands**. Boats go from Phuket daily and the trip south lasts two hours. Day tours will take you to the Viking Cave and to beautiful Maya Bay. Do spend a night there if possible, so you will have time to enjoy some of the most incredible scenery in the country. Underwater enthusiasts can explore some of the richest marine life found in the Andaman Sea.

Patong Beach on Phuket is paradise to anyone from colder climes, but it's not the best place for peace and quiet.

Fish are not the only attraction, either, for high up in the sea cliffs lives a vast number of sea swallows. The nests that the birds build so industriously at great heights are collected at considerable risk by the islanders—it's a profitable export business, supplying Chinese restaurants with the raw material for that great, but expensive delicacy, bird's nest soup. Locals believe that the soup will provide a cure for skin and lung problems as well as impotence and loss of appetite. Such is the demand that some nests fetch prices as high as 1,000 U.S. dollars.

An underground cave at Phangnga, the spectacular, limestone-studded bay northeast of Phuket.

Closer to Phuket—and considerably cheaper—is the popular **Naga Noi Pearl Farm**, which can be visited by half-day excursion. This is home to the biggest cultivated pearl in the world, weighing a massive 30 grams (1 ounce). Boats carry groups of tourists to the island daily to watch the pearl cultivation and after lunch will drop you back at your hotel.

☞ Ko Samui

Backpackers long ago thought that they could keep Ko Samui secret. However, this tropical, palm-fringed island, just three hours from the busy seaport town of Surat Thani, has become one of the best-known havens in the south, with idyllic hotels and bungalows and even an airport. Not that that has necessarily spoiled the laid-back feel of the place, for people are still coming here to laze on the beaches, eat excellent seafood, visit the surrounding islands—and most of all just to get away from the hustle and bustle.

Honeymooners and comfort seekers often stay on Chaweng Beach, which is arguably the most beautiful stretch, packed with restaurants and discos. If you want something more exclusive, try peaceful Choeng Mon Beach. For the pick of the cheaper hotels and bungalows, head for Lamai to the south.

A host of beach sports is offered, as well as tennis, water-fall trips, and even an excursion to a coconut-picking farm. For an afternoon diversion, you can also rent a motorcycle or jeep to tour the island. The road follows the coast almost all the way round, though you should stop off at Lamai to visit the intriguing museum and see the odd-shaped rocks known universally as "grandfather rocks." Remember that the roads are steep—and tourists with grazed knees are by no means an uncommon sight. A safer means of transport is a *songthaew*, but they only run until 6:00 P.M.

There are daily flights from Bangkok to Ko Samui, taking just 50 minutes. Buses take 15 hours, while trains run to Surat Thani, from where it is 2 hours by boat to Ko Samui.

Hat Yai

More than two-thirds of the way down the southern coast, and half an hour's drive inland, you will come to a town best known for sex and smuggling. Hat Yai is the fastest-growing provincial capital in the country, and as such has to deal with the crowds of Malaysians who cross the border daily for cheap shopping and sinning.

Visit the market off Niphat Uthit Road, where at the snake stalls you can drink a pint of snakes' blood, mixed with a little alcohol or honey. At **Wat Hat Yai Nal** you can get right into the abdomen of a giant reclining Buddha to explore the sculpted heart and lungs, which are said to hold a relic of the Buddha.

An exotic daytime attraction takes place on the first or second Sunday of each month: bullfighting Thai style. In this, Thai bulls lock horns in a tenacious struggle for superiority, and the slightest indication of movement animates the audience. Gamblers, who make up the vast majority of the crowd, explode in yells of encouragement, until a combatant sends a silent signal of surrender and backs away. Visitors with no sporting interest in these proceedings will find eight hours a bit much, but it's worth staying for one or two matches.

Songkhla

Although Songkhla has never been known for its nightlife, this sleepy town—which is situated 30 km (18½ miles) northeast of Hat Yai and is the very antithesis of its neighbour—offers a wide range of other attractions, amongst them lakes, beaches, and grand ramparts.

Quiet, dignified, and charming, Songkhla has a surprising history of colour and intrigue. For centuries it was an important commercial centre, part of the strong Srivijaya kingdom which ruled much of maritime Southeast Asia, but in 1654 it declared itself an independent state from Ayutthaya. Its independence didn't last, however, for in 1679 King Narai the Great of Ayutthaya attacked it and left it virtually abandoned.

Even though the white sand beaches here go on for miles, swimming is not good and the season is short. It's better to walk along the shady waterfront or to lunch at the outdoor seafood restaurants.

This quiet port in Songkhla is indicative of this sleepy town.

On the eastern side of the peninsula, where Thailand's biggest lake meets the sea, the port of Songkhla is as colourful as its red, blue, and green trawlers. You can watch these landing giant prawns, then follow the seafood to market.

For cultural interest, try the National Museum, which is over a century old and houses collections of local archaeological finds, old furniture, and items from the prehistoric site of Ban Chiang. Also, on Red Mountain, parts of the old fort, with its 18 turrets, can be seen.

Ornithologists will want to see one of southern Thailand's greatest bird parks, though this entails a two-hour journey north of town in order to get there. More than 100 different bird species can be found at **Khu Khut**, including a variety of ducks and kingfishers. The way to see them is by renting long-tailed boats. It is best to go during the early morning or late afternoon, since during the middle of the day you will be roasted by the heat.

Angkor Wat —the most imposing monument in the capital of the Khmer Empire.

☛ ANGKOR WAT (CAMBODIA)

An hour and a quarter's flight from Bangkok will get you to one of the great wonders of the world. Angkor Wat, about eight-hundred years old, is far more than just another temple; it is a vast and spectacular work of art which stands as a monument to the incredible achievements of a distant civilization.

To get there you will have to change planes in the Cambodian capital of Phnom Penh (and put up with the uncertainties of the local airline); still, the rewards of such a trip are worth any delays.

It was Henri Mouhot, the 19th-century French naturalist, who first discovered the glories of Angkor, when exploring the country as part of a trip which also took in Siam and Laos. Up until a few years ago, the site was cut off by wars and instability. Now it can be visited once again, though it is advisable to enquire about the situation with travel agents some weeks prior to departure.

Most tours will begin at the French colonial–style town of Siem Reap, with its spattering of markets, hotels, and restaurants. From here it's just a 20-minute bus ride to the fabled towers of Angkor Wat, which are visible above the treetops.

Before looking around the sprawling, ancient capital, you will probably go to **Angkor Thom**, a 12th-century walled and moated Khmer city. The entrance used by the bus is one of five ceremonial gates that are overlooked by huge stone faces of the Compassionate Bodhisattva, a deity of one of the Buddhist sects. At the very centre of the enclave is **The Bayon**, a temple so big that, as you explore it, you are liable to end up by yourself, with nobody for company but the awesome face of an idol. Bas-reliefs and voluptuous statues are among the details that have survived invasions and the elements.

Angkor Thom also contains the **Terrace of the Elephants**, where stone bas-reliefs depict elephants at peace and war. An elegant stone causeway, wide enough for a parade, leads to the main gate of **Angkor Wat**, a royal mausoleum built by the Khmer Suryavarman II, who reigned from 1113 to 1150. Its splendid galleries, courtyards, halls, and pavilions are beyond expectation. You can climb to the top of the central pyramid and look down over the entire establishment, then study in detail the intricate sandstone carvings, with their powerful Khmer images of the Buddha and other deities.

Every corner, every flight of steps, reveals a new perspective. Wander through the cool, quiet cloisters which could belong to a Mediterranean monastery, reflect on the creative power which inspired so great an edifice, or look out over the vast lotus ponds and the the surrounding jungle.

WHAT TO DO

Thailand offers an unbeatable choice of indoor and out-door activities, even if the heat is such that sometimes all you want is a swim. Most T.A.T. (Tourism Authority of Thailand) offices distribute leaflets which list details of the various activities. If you find you're lucky enough to be in Thailand at the time of a major festival, make sure that you don't miss one of the country's most joyous occasions.

FOLKLORE

The traditional *manohra* dancers and wonderful, twanging instruments are the nation's most prized gift from antiquity. You might be fortunate enough to see them at village fêtes or even at weddings and funerals, though nowadays they are more common at special tourist shows, in which the highlights are condensed and explained for the sake of neophytes. Such performances are usually accompanied by a banquet of Thai food, which renders the experience doubly pleasant.

Thai martial arts performed at these tourist shows include battles using sharp swords and sticks. The ritual which should always precede the bout involves the fighters kneeling to pay homage to their instructors and to invoke the help of the spirits, all done to the accompaniment of reed pipes and drums.

SPORTS

In Thailand's tropical swelter it would be madness to exert oneself under the midday sun. Still, there are plenty of things to do, either as a participant or as an observer, and both the T.A.T. and the local press detail activities as well as useful contact numbers.

Watersports

With some of the most beautiful waters in the Far East, it is little wonder that Thailand has become a beach-lover's paradise. Once you have finished sunning yourself, though, there is no shortage of other activities.

Sailboats are available for hire at various beaches, as are other types of vehicles, such as pedal boats and speedy little water scooters.

Fishing has only been exploited recently as a sport in Thailand, but now Bang Saray has become something of the "headquarters," although good catches of sailfish, marlin, and shark have been made by several specialists in Pattaya. If all you want is a day relaxing on deck with a rod to tempt snapper, mackerel, or parrotfish, it can easily be arranged.

Exquisite movement: graceful Thai dance was traditionally only performed in front of kings.

Scuba diving is practised at most of the major resorts, and lessons are also offered. If you have five days to devote to it, you can progress from beginner to internationally certified undersea diver.

Water-ski fans will find the required equipment and powerful boats at popular beaches.

Windsurfing requires a great deal of coordination, but worthwhile instruction is offered (allow 15 hours for a diploma).

Other Sports

If you prefer to keep your feet on the shore, there are plenty of other sports to consider.

Horse racing at Bangkok's two royal racetracks is held on most Saturdays and Sundays.

Golf lovers will soon realize that Thailand offers some fine golfing, with several top-class courses around Bangkok and Pattaya, and more being built in other tourist areas.

For the biggest knock-out sport, you just can't beat **Thai boxing**. This unique sport may be seen at folklore shows or at stadiums in Bangkok and other towns. Only kangaroos could outdo these agile punchers and kickers, who, as well as using gloved fists, fight with their elbows, knees, and feet to battle it out. Good seats are quite expensive, while third-class seats offer the excitement of spirited betting, music, and ritual. Get there early to take your pick.

SHOPPING

From the moment you reach Thailand you'll be astounded by the wealth of things to buy. Items range from stunning silk products to wooden bowls and silver earrings, from transportable goods such as textiles and clothes to fine woodwork and fragile, colourful pots. Whatever you want, Bangkok will provide you with something to fit the bill—with the notable exception of electronics, for which you would be better advised to visit Singapore.

Phuket caters to all tastes when it comes to watersports; hire a jet ski and take off into the blue.

Nor is Bangkok the only option. Chiang Mai is renowned for its handicrafts, while even the smaller towns in the north-east of the country boast their own specialities.

Tips for Shoppers

Remember that bargaining is the rule just about everywhere, apart from supermarkets and hotels—with even the large, upscale boutiques occasionally being amenable to a little bit of negotiation.

Conversely, you should also keep in mind that while fixed prices may sometimes be more expensive, they can still offer excellent value, and come with the added bonus of some form of guarantee. Sukhumvit Road in Bangkok is crammed with large, modern shopping plazas and department stores where there is no shortage of either imported or local offerings. It makes sense to wait to do your main shopping at the end of your holiday, so that you don't have to carry purchases around with you—and you'll also have a better idea by then of what you want to take home.

In Bangkok, try to plan your shopping expeditions to avoid unnecessary travel, since traffic jams make travelling round the city time-consuming, hot, and hazardous to your health.

Markets

Air-conditioned shops might sound like the best idea in the big cities, but it is the local markets that offer the real bargains. They are definitely worth a visit, if only to see the crowds and experience the excitement. Don't forget to bring a camera and to get there early, since many are like ghost towns by the middle of the day.

One of the biggest, most diverse, and best-known markets in Bangkok is the **Chatuchak Weekend Market** (see page 35). Fruit, vegetables, and spices all vie for space with pastes and food concoctions you've probably never come across before. As for take-home curios, you might like a brass temple bell, a carved buffalo horn, hill-tribe embroidered clothing, or hand-made silver jewellery. You'll also find silk flowers, batik, a variety of modern T-shirts with startling "almost English" slogans, straw baskets, and a mixture of oddities from Malaysia, India, Nepal, and Burma.

The weekday equivalent of Chatuchak can be found at the Thieves Market, Pahurat, and Chinatown, all located within easy reach of one another.

Chinatown is worth a visit simply for the sightseeing. The emphasis here is on goods with a Chinese flavour or origin, and one exotic possibility is to visit the perfume man, who'll make up a scent to please your nose while you wait.

The **Thieves Market** has a wide range of curios, some of them antique. Remember, you need an export certificate for genuine items (see page 108).

For sumptuous silks, clothing, cloth, and delicate batiks, the bargains are to be found in **Pahurat Market**. Here, products from India and Malaysia are sold alongside local items.

Another market worth visiting is **Klong Toey Market**, where you'll find a wide range of culinary items, clothing, and electrical goods at low prices.

Finally, if you like to combine your shopping with your nightlife, head for Patpong, the notorious red-light district. Private services are for sale in discos and clubs and the streets are packed with stalls. A great many of the items for sale are "genuine" imitations. Haggling is essential.

Best Buys

Antiques. If you qualify as an informed collector, then you'll find worthwhile objects from Thailand, Burma, China, Laos, and Cambodia at the Thieves' Market, in smarter shops, or in the provinces. Experts at the National Museum in Bangkok meet with the public on both Sundays and Mondays, when they vouch for the authenticity of works of art and antiquity. Don't forget—export permission is required for taking genuine antiques or art treasures out of the country (see page 108).

Art. Paintings in several media by Thai artists, usually on familiar rice paddy or temple spire themes, are sold in galleries and shops all over the main towns. Temple stone rubbings on rice paper are another typical souvenir.

Artificial flowers. As well as cultivating some of the world's most beautiful flowers, Thailand also exports large quantities of hand-made imitations.

Bronze. A great Thai tradition, which is now used for tableware in addition to lamps, bells, candelabra, and statues.

Ceramics. A particular wood is used in the kilns to bake *celadon*, a distinctive Thai pottery. Porcelain is also made in Thailand. Ming and Ching dynasty bowls and shards turn up, salvaged from the river at Ayutthaya and Sukhothai.

Dolls. Including hilltribe costumes, Thai dancers, and peasant women in *sampans.*

Elephants. This favourite Thai symbol is often immortalized in wood carvings, thumb-sized to life-sized, in jade and in flashy models studded with glass.

The Art of Bargaining

Want a natty wooden elephant, a lurid leather bag, or even a ride in a taxi? Then remember to bargain for it. First ask how much the price is. Then name a figure considerably lower and somewhat less than you are prepared to pay, and eventually agree on a compromise. A few hints to help out: always check the prices on several stalls to get an idea of the cost; don't be misled by sweet smiles and sob stories—and remember, at the end of the day, so long as you are happy with the price you've got a bargain.

Fashion. Clothes to order—allegedly in 24 hours or less—can be a solid bargain in Thailand, but try to give the tailor several days if you want a first-rate garment. Trousers, dresses, suits, shirts, and bikinis can all be made to measure. Women's ready-to-wear shops often sell good, cheap local copies of the latest European fashions. Tropical sports shirts may also be bought off the peg (ready-made).

Gems. Precious stones such as sapphires and rubies are mined in Thailand, while others are imported at favourable prices from Burma, India, Sri Lanka, and other countries. Bangkok claims to be the world's top gem-cutting centre. Seek out a reputable shop and try to avoid unrealistic bargains: fakes are very common.

Handicrafts. With great skill, patience, and ingenuity, the artisans of Thailand produce an apparently endless variety of hand-crafted objects. Each region has its specialities.

Ivory. Chinese-style elephant sculptures, Mandarin figurines, as well as incredible one-piece globe-within-globe follies.

Jewellery. Thai designers tend towards traditional styles, but originals can be ordered. Pick carefully where you shop; the establishments which cater to tour buses often pay the travel agency a 20 percent kickback on what you spend. Thai costume jewellery can be cheap.

> It is illegal to take Buddha images out of Thailand unless prior permission has been given.

Kites: Fighting models, neatly folded, make an original gift.

Lacquerware. Pretty gold-and-black boxes in the shape of fantasy animals.

Mobiles. Cheerful hanging ensembles; bells made of shell.

Nielloware. Black metal alloy inlaid on silver for trinkets.

Old books. Look for old Burmese manuscripts—on parchment, illuminated, and bound in leather.

The artisans of Chiang Mai weave a variety of handicrafts.

Pottery. A typical Thai variety—*benjarong* ware—has a five-coloured design on a background of grey, white, or black. Also, patterned porcelain jars, plates, pots, even spitoons.

Rattan goods. Lightweight furniture; peasant hats.

Seashells. Notable bargains at Thai beach resorts, in shops or from itinerant vendors.

Tape cassettes. Both Thai and international pop and classical music at bargain prices. Pirate tapes are not common.

Thai silk and fabrics. Happy silkworms keep thousands of nimble weavers busy, hand and foot, in producing the famous, colourful Thai fabrics. Ranging from lightweight blouses to heavy bedspreads, the long-lasting fabrics live up to their worldwide reputation. Durable Thai cotton, most of which is factory made, goes into ready-to-wear clothing, towels, some toys, and tablecloths. Keep an eye open for brightly coloured padded jackets.

Umbrellas. All around Chiang Mai, locals make hand-painted parasols—to your own design, if you wish.

Wood carvings. Figurines, teak furniture, salad bowls, and a variety of other knick-knacks.

Xylophones. The Thai versions, known as *ranad ek* and *ranad thum* (treble and alto respectively), have wooden bars on a boat-shaped soundbox.

Zoological curiosities. Moths and butterflies with Latin captions; stuffed cobras poised to strike; stuffed mongooses as opponents.

ENTERTAINMENT

Mention Bangkok to anybody and the chances are they'll ask you about the city's nightlife. Indeed, from nightclubs to go-go bars, Thailand hums with excitement—even early birds will not be able to miss it.

There are also a few quieter things to do for family entertainment. Nightclubs, mostly in the major hotels, feature live bands, floor shows, and dancing. Bangkok offers discotheques, as well as more intimate places where combo or piano music is played, plus bars and pubs for friendly conversation.

Various nightclub-style restaurants specialize in traditional Thai food and music; the floor show consists of performances by Thai dancers, regional folklore, or both.

Otherwise, cultural possibilities suitable for foreign visitors are quite limited. Visiting musicians sometimes perform, as do local theatre groups. Due to a stiff tax on imported films, very few foreign imports are shown. This is supposed to encourage the Thai film industry, which still produces a constant stream of second-rate movies. Some bars, clubs, hotels, and even a few associations fill the gap by showing imported films on a semi-private basis.

The Go-Go Scene

In just Bangkok alone you can choose from several hundred nightclubs and go-go bars, and throughout the country several thousand more. These, along with the thousands of escorts and dancers who work in them, cater to every taste, from easy conversation to the unabashed hedonism of the girlie bars and the mind-boggling acrobatics of the upstairs bars. Although they are obviously aimed at single, heterosexual males, women are usually welcome to come in for a drink and a look. Gay bars are increasingly run in the same areas, particularly in Bangkok and Chiang Mai.

A neon-studded street in Bangkok is lined with nightclubs and restaurants.

In Patpong—usually seen as the best-known red-light area of the lot (more people visit it every year than the Grand Palace)—there are even markets, pizza shops, and Thai boxing displays for entertainment.

Before you go, remember a few words of warning. Upstairs bars are frequently a front for live sex shows and may try to charge vast amounts of money. Wise people always check the price before entering a bar; if there is trouble, simply pay the bill and get in touch with the tourist police. Pimps, including many taxi drivers, are good at making enticing suggestions which, were you to take them up, would usually be more expensive than you would anticipate. Touts who hang around outside hotels and bars know where to find live sex shows and other pornographic diversions. However, strictly speaking, these are illegal and could be raided by the police.

Women, too, are not always what they seem—transvestites might well give macho clients more than they bargained for. AIDS and other venereal diseases are also rife (just count the number of venereal disease clinics).

Provincial nightlife is often calmer than that in the capital, though many towns have nightclubs with hostesses for hire, massage parlours, and the like. Pattaya has a comprehensive nightlife comparing favourably with Bangkok's. Down in the far south, Hat Yai outdoes all other provincial towns with a highly concentrated entertainment zone.

Festivals and Holidays

The list below details only a few of the principal events that have made Thailand renowned as one of the Far East's most colourful nations. Check dates before you leave, however, as many depend on the position of the sun or the moon.

February: Flower carnival in Chiang Mai. Floats; parades.

April: The Songkran, or Water Festival, is most uninhibitedly celebrated in Chiang Mai, but is also fun in Bangkok.

May: The timing of the Royal Ploughing Ceremony is determined by the king's Brahmin astrologers, and comes just before the rainy season. The king presides over the ceremonies at Sanam Luang, Bangkok (a field across from Wat Phra Kaeo).

May: Bun Bong Fai (rocket) festival. Drums, dances, fireworks. Mostly in the northeast.

July: *Asanha Puja*. Candlelit processions by full moon at every temple in Thailand.

October–November: The end of the rainy season and Buddhist Lent comes with Kathin; processions bear gifts of robes and utensils to the monks.

November: *Loi Krathong*, at the full moon; candles and incense are floated down canals on banana-leaf boats, notably in Bangkok and Chiang Mai. Also, the elephant round-up in Surin in the northeast, when T.A.T. and provincial authorities move hundreds of elephants.

EATING OUT

Good food in Thailand is as ubiquitous as beaches—and often quite a lot hotter besides. If you don't like chillies, don't give up on the food. *Mai phet* (not hot), stressed at the time you order, can bring a delicious selection of cooler, more subtle flavours that may include any taste from the sweetness of coconut milk to the pungency of fresh herbs, lemon grass, garlic, or nutmeg and the saltiness of fermented fish. Added to that are tropical fruits such as fresh pineapple, a little sugar, a pinch of coriander—and, of course, a lashing of culinary inspiration.

Every region boasts its own gastronomical specialties. Up in the north, a local sausage known as *naem* is popular, while the northeast is famed for its sticky or glutinous rice (*khao nia*), normally served as an accompaniment to barbecued meat (generally buffalo), as well as *som tam*, a tasty hot salad that combines shredded green papaya with dried shrimps or curried crab claws, lemon juice, garlic, fish sauce, and chillies.

The south produces numerous dishes that have been influenced by the Muslim style of cooking of the Malays and, of course, all kinds of seafood dishes, including crab, squid, shark, freshly cooked lobsters, and mussels.

Don't worry if you have a sweet tooth—you're not likely to go hungry at all.

Many Thai sweets are based on rice flour, coconut milk, palm sugar, and sticky rice, and just about all of them are delicious.

Menus are not usually displayed outside of restaurants.

WHAT TO EAT

If you are a newcomer to Thai food, start off with something mild (*mai*

phet) and then work up to pig's intestine soup or chillied serpents' heads! Also good to start with are curries (*kaeng phet*)—particularly those with a coconut cream base, which are less piquant than Indian varieties—and there is never any shortage of wonderful fresh fish.

The ingredients to Thailand's exotic dishes can be found in local food stalls.

When eating chillies, take a local tip and have plenty of steamed rice, which helps to soothe the stomach and will smother the fire. Nothing else is as effective, and cold drinks are certainly one of the worst antidotes possible.

Appetizers: *Paw pia tod* is a Thai spring roll enclosing a sweet-and-sour bean sprouts, pork, and crabmeat.

Gai hor bai toey consists of chicken chunks fried with sesame oil, soya sauce, oyster sauce, herbs, and a drop of whisky, all in a leaf wrapper.

Soup: *Tom yam* is a hot-sour soup, made with either pork, shrimp, beef, chicken or fish, which must be accompanied by plenty of steamed rice to soak up the excess chilli heat. Note the fanciful selection of herbs and leaves which are left floating in the big bowl.

Gaeng jeud is a less pungent soup made from chicken, pork, and shrimp cooked with Chinese-style vegetables and Thai herbs and spices.

Rice and noodles: *Kao pad* is fried rice with bits of meat.

Mee grob is crispy fried rice noodles with pork, egg, bean sprouts, shrimp, and a sweet-and-sour flavour.

Bah mee nam is a rich broth of thin noodles, pork, or chicken chunks, mixed with herbs, bean sprouts, and subtle spices. This is a filling soup which could serve as a main dish.

Seafood: *Hor mok pla* is a fish curry with vegetables and coconut milk, served wrapped in banana leaves.

Pla preow wan is fried fish covered in a thick sweet-and-sour sauce.

Gung tod—or crispy fried prawns—usually comes with a choice of sauces.

Meat: *Gaeng mud-sa-man* is a beef curry less spicy than most, and has an overtone of peanuts.

Kao nah gai is sliced chicken with spring onion, bamboo shoots, and steamed rice.

Sa lad neua san translates as roast beef salad and contains vegetables, chillies, garlic, and perhaps mint.

Sweets: *Salim* is a refreshing sweet of sugared noodles with coconut milk and crushed ice.

Ice cream, pronounced *eye-cream,* sometimes comes in original and natural flavors. A local variation of a sundae, for instance, is coconut ice cream sprinkled with peanuts and kernels of corn.

Fruit: *Somo*, meaning pomelo, is something akin to a tropical cousin of the grapefruit and is served divided into sections.

Sap-pa-rot, pineapple, is a familiar fruit but twice as tasty on its home ground. More exotic local fruits are rarely on restaurant menus, but can be discovered at markets and on street stalls. Just point if you don't know the name.

Ngor (rambutan) looks like an overdeveloped hairy strawberry; the fruit is inside.

Lamut, a light-brown fruit that has to be peeled, is syrupy sweet, with a taste reminiscent of fresh figs.

Durian, that monster with spiky thorns, contains bits of custard-like fruit around egg-shaped piths; its smell is often thought to be more oppressive than a rubbish heap.

Try delicious local oranges, bananas, mangoes, papayas —almost every fruit imaginable, except apples and pears, which don't grow here and are imported and expensive.

Curiosities

There is no need to hold back on quantity or restrict yourself to one dish, for Thais will generally order a selection and share them as a group.

Thai restaurants often welcome customers with cold, and even sometimes frozen, hand towels, as a relief from the tropical world outside. Many restaurants have also taken to issuing disposable mini-towels in small plastic packets; the explosions you hear all about you are the Thais smacking the air-tight packs to open them.

In cheaper restaurants the bill is calculated by the number of plates sitting on the table in front of you and will be given to you verbally.

Don't expect to find knives on Thai tables—a spoon is used instead. Salt and pepper cellars (shakers) will also be absent—the piquancy of the food is such that it is unlikely you'll need them. A few sauces may be offered, however.

Nam prik, "pepper water," is a much-prized concoction of pounded red chillies, shrimp paste, black pepper, garlic, and onions mixed with tamarind, lemon juice, ginger, and fish in an early state of fermentation.

If you do find the food undersalted, add a little *nam pla*, a caramel-coloured fish sauce with tiny chilli segments in it. Small bowls of roasted chillies, from the famous *prik kee noo*

Wandering down a back street in Bangkok, don't be surprised to find a restaurant.

("mouse-dropping pepper") to the potent *prik chii faa,* are also served on the side—for diners of a more robust constitution.

When in Asia...

For a change of both taste and scenery, try one of the various Asian restaurants that serve a spectrum of different cuisines —almost all of them at bargain prices. By far the most common non-Thai Asian cuisine is Chinese food. In Bangkok you can sample the most important regional schools of Chinese cooking—Szechuan, Canton, Shanghai, and Peking— as well as the less familiar food of the Hakka, Chiu Chow, and Hunan peoples.

Restaurants specializing in food from neighbouring Cambodia, Malaysia, Burma, and Laos are not easy to find, but more distant and better-known cuisines—like Japanese and Korean—are well represented.

For quite different reasons, including the flow of refugees, Vietnamese restaurants have become noticeably more widespread. The significant population of Thais of Indian descent or Muslim religion accounts for the availability of curries and associated foods.

Western Cuisine

Most hotels serve an approximation of European food. For greater authenticity, try out the various nationality restaurants, many in Bangkok owned by foreign residents. Among the possibilities are French, American, German, Hungarian, Italian, Scandinavian, British, and Swiss cooking.

Drinks

Iced water is frequently served at the start of a meal. It's almost bound to be safe to drink in any decent restaurant, but if in doubt ask for a bottle of water and skip the ice. Thais usually drink water or cold tea (*cha jin yen*) throughout their meal, along with whisky with dinner.

You can drink anything you please and the Thais will not be surprised: iced coffee or iced tea, soft drinks, milk, fruit juice, beer, or lemonade. Thai lemonade is normally salted to fight dehydration in the hot climate: you may not appreciate the taste, but it helps to avoid covering all your food in salt.

All wines are disastrously expensive in Thailand, costing several times the price in their country of origin. Even in a modest restaurant, an undistinguished wine could cost more than the whole dinner.

Thailand does produce good beer, though, and brand names to try are Singha, Kloster, and Amarit—all are stronger than you expect.

Thai whisky, on the other hand, is weaker and cheaper than you'd think (Mekhong is the best-known brand), though this, too, can result in frighteningly bad hangovers.

To Help You Order

Could we have a table ...?   *kor toh ...dai mai?*

I'd like a/an/some ...   *Chan yak cha ...*

beer	*beer*
beef	*neua*
bread	*kha-nome-pung*
chicken	*gai*
coffee	*kafae*
curry	*gaeng*
egg	*khai*
fish	*pla*
meat	*neua*
menu	*maynu raigarn arharn*
milk	*nom*
noodles	*kwaytio*
pork	*moo*
rice	*kao*
salt	*keua*
shrimp	*gung*
soup	*soop*
sugar	*nam thal*
tea	*cha*
water	*nam*
watermelon	*taeng-mo*

INDEX

HANDY TRAVEL TIPS

An A–Z Summary of Practical Information

A

ACCOMMODATION (See also CAMPING, YOUTH HOSTELS and RECOMMENDED HOTELS on pages 129-136)

The balance between supply and demand in Bangkok and the major tourist destinations varies enormously, but advance reservations for hotel rooms are always a good idea. Bangkok has 35,000 rooms considered suitable for foreign tourists; budget travellers will find many no-frills, native-style hotels as well. Of the former, even the cheapest are completely air-conditioned, and many have swimming pools and other comforts. International-standard hotels are also found in the beach resorts and regional capitals such as Chiang Mai and Hat Yai.

In smaller towns, facilities may be fairly basic — but so are prices.

Do you have a (double) room?   **Mee hong (kuu) mai?**

AIRPORT

Don Muang international airport (tel. 535 1254 departures; 535 1301 arrivals; 535 1111 directory assistance), 30 km (18½ miles) north of Bangkok, is Thailand's principal gateway, and the arrival and departure terminals are up to the highest international standards, with a selection of duty-free shops. Immigration and customs clearances are efficient and swift. In the arrival hall, a full range of facilities, including porters, limousine service, hotel desks, and a Tourism Authority of Thailand (T.A.T.) information bureau, is available 24 hours a day. Local telephone calls can be made free of charge from call boxes in the arrival and departure halls.

City taxis (without yellow plates) can be taken to the city centre, but airport taxis and limousines are better, safer, and more likely to have English-speaking drivers. Cheaper (for lone travellers) air-conditioned mini-buses also pick up at the terminal, but are much slower alternatives. From the airport to Bangkok's hotels takes between 45 minutes and 3 hours, depending on the traffic.

Those heading for Pattaya can take an air-conditioned coach there directly from the airport (about a three-hour trip).

Internal flights. Although buses and trains are usually comfortable, the fast (but more expensive) way to reach the far north or south is by air. Domestic airlines run a comprehensive service of jet and turbo-prop flights to all parts of the country, including Chiang Mai in the north and Ko Samui, Phuket, and Hat Yai in the south.

B

BICYCLE and MOPED HIRE

Although not advisable in the horror of Bangkok traffic, bikes can be rented at several hotels and guesthouses. At beach resorts such as Pattaya, Ko Samui, and Phuket, bikes and mopeds can be hired through your hotel reception or travel counter. Distant beaches and Chiang Mai lend themselves to exploration by bike or moped.

BOAT TRIPS (See also GUIDES and TOURS)

Guided boat tours are a pleasant, if expensive, way to see Bangkok's river and canals. For cheap, do-it-yourself sightseeing, take the river bus (baht boat) — only a few baht for an hour's trip up or down the mighty Chao Phraya. For the canals, private long-tailed boats (*hang yao*) may be rented from outside the Oriental Hotel or from river stops at the Grand Palace (Tha Chang) and Wat Po (Tha Thien).

C

CAMPING

Several national parks offer camping facilities, as do a number of the islands. Camping is not recommended outside in the wilds, as robberies and hold-ups are not uncommon.

CAR HIRE (See also DRIVING)

To rent a car you must be over 21 and hold an international driving licence. You may be asked for a deposit equal to the estimated final cost, though some companies may waive this for credit-card holders. Insurance is usually offered on a daily basis at extra cost.

Thailand

CHILDREN'S THAILAND

Children take to Thailand like ducks to water. The main problem is the heat. Bring a lot of sun screen, and ask doctors about vaccinations and other requirements. Although there is plenty to keep children amused, travel time to Bangkok attractions can involve a 2-hour drive.

CLIMATE

Thailand enjoys its best weather just when the northern temperate zone is suffering the worst of winter. November to February are the favoured months in Bangkok, ironically known as the "cool season," when the temperature dips a bit below the usual debilitating extreme and, more important, the humidity is lower. Rain is quite rare.

The following chart for Bangkok gives the average maximum and minimum daily temperatures and number of rainy days per month:

		J	F	M	A	M	J	J	A	S	O	N	D
average daily	°F	89	91	93	95	93	91	90	90	89	88	87	87
maximum	°C	32	33	34	35	34	33	32	32	32	31	31	31
average daily	°F	68	72	75	77	77	76	76	76	76	75	72	68
minimum	°C	20	22	24	25	25	25	24	24	24	24	22	20
rainy days		2	2	4	5	14	16	19	21	23	17	7	1

Although temperatures of 36–38°C (97°–100°F) are common in the hot season, widespread use of air-conditioning relieves discomfort. The rainy season (monsoon) lasts from about June to October. It rains mostly in the afternoon or evening, cooling and refreshing the tropical air, and inundating the streets.

CLOTHING

Pack for the tropics; the more cotton the better. A light sweater might come in handy if you are planning a trip to the hills; the only other place you may feel cold is in a strongly air-conditioned restaurant. Immodesty should be avoided: adults should not wear shorts when visiting temples, and women with plunging necklines will receive plenty of stares, not all admiring. The Thais are strict about covering up, except on the beach, but are quite casual as regards dressing up — even the Grand Palace no longer requires jackets and ties. Almost all restaurants and nightclubs share the same informal approach.

COMPLAINTS (See also POLICE)

If you have a dispute with a hotel, merchant, or any organization or person in Thailand, it is important not to lose your temper. If your complaint has no effect after you have tried approaching the person or establishment concerned directly, consult the Tourism Authority of Thailand. In serious cases, the tourist police can often be of assistance in resolving the problem.

CRIME (See also EMERGENCIES)

Beware of pickpockets in crowded marketplaces. Purse-snatchers are now motorized in Bangkok, fleeing on a motorbike almost before the victim realizes what's happened. Don't tempt bandits by flaunting jewels or ostentatious clothes, and never leave irreplaceable items in your hotel room; use the safe-deposit box, but get an official receipt. At seaside resorts, never leave any valuables on the beach when you go swimming. At Phuket, the authorities advise tourists to avoid isolated beaches, where they might be accosted by robbers.

CUSTOMS and ENTRY FORMALITIES (See also MEDICAL CARE)

Citizens of most countries need tourist visas to stay more than 30 days in Thailand. For the latest regulations, check with your travel agent or the Thai consulate in your own country. So-called undesirable tourists — meaning presumed "hippies"— may be refused entry, or required to prove financial responsibility. Any visitor may be asked to prove his or her solvency by producing the equivalent of Bt 10,000 (per person) or Bt 20,000 (per family) upon arrival (in currency, traveller's cheques, or credit cards).

Duty Free. On entering Thailand, you may take in 200 cigarettes *or* 250 cigars *or* 250g tobacco, plus one litre of *either* spirits *or* wine.

Thailand

Currency restrictions. There is no restriction on the import of foreign currency, but amounts over the equivalent of 10,000 U.S. dollars must be declared. On leaving the country, you may take out up to 10,000 U.S. dollars or the equivalent in foreign currency (more if declared on arrival). Gold jewellery and video cameras must also be declared when you arrive.

When leaving Thailand, note that the export of any images of Buddha or other deities is prohibited. It is also prohibited to export antiquities without special permission from the Fine Arts Department. Some shops will be able to handle this for you. Alternatively, you can contact the office directly:

National Museum, Fine Arts Department, 4 Na Phra That Road, Bangkok; tel. 224 1370.

D

DRIVING

As in many Asian countries, traffic in Thailand is supposed to keep to the left. Due to chronic traffic jams, driving conditions in the Bangkok metropolis are appalling; peak traffic persists almost all day, with only brief periods of respite. On the main highways out of town, free-spirited drivers make up their own rules as they go along, using whatever part of the road they feel they need, even if it means running another car into a ditch. As you discover the local driving customs, you won't need reminding to stay extremely alert. Watch out, too, for buses in one-way streets going in the opposite direction to traffic. The official speed limit is 40 km/h (25 mph) in towns, 80 km/h (50 mph) on highways.

Fuel and oil. Readily available in both regular and super.

Breakdowns. Telephone the rental firm from which you hired the car to come and rescue you. In an emergency dial the Highway Police Patrol Centre; tel. 193.

Parking. Car parks (parking lots) and metered parking are found on some streets.

Road signs. Many Thai road signs are standard international pictographs. Speed limits are always posted in Arabic numerals.

Accident	**u bat hed**
Collision	**rod chon**
Flat tyre	**yang bean**
Help!	**chuey duey!**
Police!	**tam ruat!**

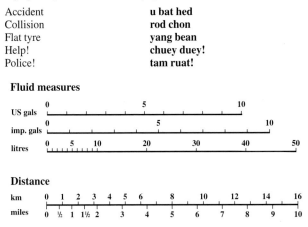

Fluid measures

Distance

DRUGS

Most of the big narcotics arrests in Thailand involve people caught trying to smuggle drugs out for sale abroad. Possession of heroin or its variants for trade and distribution is punishable by five years to life imprisonment (foreigners), death sentence (Thais), and a fine of up to half a million baht. Possessing, trading, or smoking of marijuana or related substances is punishable by as much as six months in prison. Ignorance of Thai law is not a mitigating factor in drug cases.

E

ELECTRIC CURRENT

The standard current in Thailand is 220-volt, 50-cycle AC; most hotel rooms have an electrical outlet for shavers; some have 110-volt sockets too.

Thailand

EMBASSIES and CONSULATES

For a complete list of embassies and consulates see the yellow pages of the Bangkok telephone directory under "Embassies, Consulates & Legations." For Thai visa problems, consult the Tourism Authority of Thailand or the Immigration Division; tel. 287 3101 up to 3110.

Australia: 37 Sathon Tai Road; tel. 287 2680; 8am–12:30pm and 1:45–4pm Monday to Friday.

Canada: Boonmitr Building, 11th & 12th floors, 138 Silom Road; tel. 237 4125/6; visa section 9:30am–12pm Monday to Thursday; Friday all sections 7:30am–1pm.

Ireland: United Flour Mill Building, 11th floor, 105 Rajawongse Road; tel. 223 0876, 223 0470/9; 9am–12pm and 1:30–4pm Monday to Friday.

Japan: 1674 New Phetburi Road; tel. 252 6151/9.

New Zealand: 93 Witthayu Road; tel. 251 8165; 8am–12pm and 1–4pm Monday to Friday.

United Kingdom: 1031 Ploenchit Road; tel. 253 0191/9; 8am–11am, 1–3:30pm Monday to Thursday, 8am–12pm Friday.

U.S.A.: 95 Witthayu Road; tel. 205 4000; 7:30am–12pm and 1– 4pm Monday to Friday.

EMERGENCIES

The main hospitals treat urgent medical problems 24 hours a day; below are some useful telephone numbers:

Bangkok General Hospital	318 0066
Bangkok Adventist Hospital	281 1422
Prommitr Hospital	259 0373/8
Police Hospital, Rama I Road	252 8111 up to 25 (accidents only)

Provincial towns also have fully equipped hospitals.

The following numbers may also be useful in an emergency:

Tourist Assistance Centre (Bangkok)	282 8129, 281 5051
Highway Police Patrol Centre	193
Fire	199 or Bangkok: 246 0199
Ambulance	252 2171/5
All-purpose emergency number	**191**

ETIQUETTE

Ignorance of Thai sensibilities can cause much embarrassment. The monarchy is greatly revered, so the slightest indication of disrespect, even accidental, could have serious consequences. This even applies to money bearing the king's likeness.

Religion plays a most important part in the life of the Thais. When you visit a temple, dress soberly — no shorts or revealing blouses. Wear shoes, but you must remove them before entering the chapel. Never show disrespect to a religious object or to Buddhist monks and nuns (don't offer money to a monk, but you can offer a cigarette). Women are not allowed in certain temples nor should they touch monks or novices or hand anything directly to them.

Note that since the head is considered sacred, you must not touch anyone there. Don't point your feet towards another person's body (remember this especially in temples, where you'll see worshippers' feet tucked behind them), and don't use them to open a door. Don't lose your temper or display strong emotion (including boisterous thanks). Finally, in spite of Bangkok's reputation, public displays of affection between the sexes are frowned upon.

Remember, Thailand may be known as the "Land of Smiles," but a smile can just as easily conceal disapproval as imply acceptance.

G

GETTING TO THAILAND

Because of the complexity and variety of fares available, you should ask the advice of an informed travel agent well before departure.

Thailand

By Air

Scheduled flights. Bangkok's Don Muang international airport (see AIRPORTS) is the principal gateway to Thailand and a major airport of entry to the Far East. Regular services arrive from Europe, America, Canada, Australia, and Asia. The flight from London takes roughly 14 hours, from New York 24 hours, from Sydney 13 hours.

Charter flights and package tours. *From the U.K. and Ireland*: a wide range of package tours to Thailand, or tours featuring Thailand as part of a package, are available. Among the most popular is the "fly-cruise": you fly to Bangkok or Singapore, then cruise from there to Bali, Jakarta, and other Far Eastern ports. *From North America*: Several tour operators offer Group Inclusive Tour (G.I.T.) programmes that feature Bangkok along with other exotic ports of call in Asia. From 15 to 30 days in length, these tours include air transport between scheduled cities, transfers to and from hotels, hotel accommodation, some sightseeing, and the services of an English-speaking guide, some or all meals, as well as tips and service charges. These G.I.T.s may be extended to include a stop-over in Hawaii.

By Road

Private car travel to Thailand is almost impossible, as the Burmese border is closed. Cars can be driven in from Malaysia and Singapore.

By Rail

From Singapore, trains travel through Malaysia to Bangkok, including the new luxury service run by the world-famous Venice-Simplon Orient Express, known as the Eastern and Oriental Express.

GUIDES and TOURS

The enterprising Bangkok travel trade has devised scores of excursions for tourists, from the floating market boat trip to archaeological outings. Nine pages of agencies are listed in the classified telephone directory under "Travel Bureaux." For interpreters, see the entry "Translators and Interpreters" in the *Yellow Pages*. Avoid unauthorized guides who greet you on the street and offer to show you Bangkok (see TOUTS).

H

HELPLINES

Disabled travellers. Although lift services are available in all big hotels, and wheelchairs can be found at local airports, facilities for disabled travellers are few and far between. For further information contact the Association for the Disabled in Bangkok, tel. 463 5929.

Women travelling alone. Precautions apply as for any country or city. Main tourist areas are safe, and you shouldn't stray from these on your own at night. On arrival to any main city in Thailand, go to the Tourist Assistance Centre, which will be able to advise and help you.

Gay & Lesbian. Thailand does not openly accept homosexuality, though it does tolerate it. *Utopia*, a gay and lesbian cultural and information centre, can be contacted at 259 9619.

L

LANGUAGE (See also USEFUL EXPRESSIONS on pages 127-128)

Although English is widely used in hotels and shops — it's the best-known Western language in Thailand — try to express some simple phrases in Thai. The Thai language spoken in Bangkok is understood everywhere in the country, though there are many dialects and sub-dialects. In addition, several other languages are widely used, such as Lao in the northeast, Malay in the south, and the Teochiu dialect of Chinese in many different areas. Like Chinese, Thai uses intonation to distinguish between otherwise identical words, which makes it a difficult language for foreigners. Each syllable can have up to five different meanings depending on how it is pronounced; there are 44 consonants plus dozens of vowels, compounds, and tone marks. If all this doesn't discourage you, consider Rachasap, a special language used only when speaking to or about Thai royalty!

Try to imitate a Thai to learn how to intone these useful words; your efforts will be appreciated by everyone you meet. You will find a list of useful expressions on the cover of this guide.

LAUNDRY and DRY CLEANING

Many hotels will take care of your laundry for you, returning it within 24 hours and even within 4 hours at premium rates. Dry cleaning takes two days unless "express service" is specified, when it takes half the time but costs 50 percent extra. Laundries and dry cleaners are listed under "Laundries" in the classified telephone directory. There are some semi-self-service laundrettes in Thailand.

LOST PROPERTY

If you lose something, check with your hotel receptionist, then report the loss to the nearest police station or, in Bangkok, to the Tourist Assistance Centre (see TOURIST INFORMATION OFFICES).

M

MAPS

The Tourism Authority of Thailand issues free bus and tourist maps showing the principal attractions of Bangkok. These aren't always adequate, though, and it is better to buy one of the commercially produced maps of Bangkok and Thailand that are sold at hotels and bookshops. Interesting specialized maps of the waterways and markets of Bangkok are also available.

MEDICAL CARE

Don't let the heat get you down. If you are not used to the tropics, respect the midday sun; it can broil you in an hour. To avoid dehydration, have plenty of salt on your breakfast eggs (the Thais put salt in their lemonade). Spare your digestive system by experimenting gradually until you're more accustomed to the spicy Thai cuisine. Wear light, airy clothing and a hat in the sun, and don't go anywhere barefoot (because of snakes).

Check with your doctor before leaving home for recommendations on **malaria** prevention. While Bangkok and other principal towns are malaria-free, the disease can be found in some parts of Thailand. Hotels often have doctors on call; alternatively, look one up in the classified (yellow) pages of the telephone directory under "Physicians and Surgeons."

Bangkok has efficient, modern hospitals staffed by well-qualified personnel. Since health care can be expensive, make sure you have arranged an adequate insurance policy covering illness or accident on holiday before you go.

Chemists' shops (drugstores) are open from about 9am–9pm, and later in some areas. Most foreign drugs are available, though it's wise to check the expiration date on the package. Many drugs that are normally available by prescription only can be bought over the counter. If you do decide to be your own doctor, it's worth asking for a printed advice note on the side effects of whatever drugs you buy.

I need a doctor.	**pom/chan tong karn maw.**
I need a dentist.	**pom/chan tong kan maw fang.**

Vaccinations. Visitors arriving in Thailand should have certificates proving the validity of their cholera, yellow fever, and smallpox vaccinations if they are coming from infected areas. The risk of malaria exists in rural areas all over the country. Vaccinations against both cholera and typhoid are particularly recommended. Check with your doctor well before departure for the latest information and advice.

MONEY MATTERS

The unit of currency in Thailand is the baht (abbreviated Bt or B), divided into 100 satang. Banknotes come in denominations of 10, 20, 50, 100, 500, and 1,000 baht. Coins are 25 and 50 satang, 1, 5, and 10 baht. Note that 1-baht coins are found in two different sizes (it's only the small one that can be used in most street telephones). The 5-baht coin is also available in two sizes, but can be distinguished from the large 1-baht coin by the copper streak on the edge.

A number of mini-buses have now been converted into motorized currency-exchange units. They circulate through the streets of central Bangkok, Pattaya, Phuket, and Chiang Mai.

Banks and exchange facilities. Normally the exchange rate at banks is the most favourable. After the banks are closed you can change money at your hotel, at exchange booths, or at shops displaying a sign in English saying "money changer."

Banks and money-changers in tourist towns will accept virtually any currency. There is no black market in pounds or dollars, and carrying them with you can constitute a security risk. The best way is to take traveller's cheques or use credit cards.

Credit cards. Major hotels, restaurants, and shops are accustomed to the well-known international charge cards. One or two major cards can be used in cash-withdrawal machines, but as the instructions are sometimes in Thai script, it can be easier to go inside, where you will need your passport for identification.

Prices. (See also PLANNING YOUR BUDGET, below) Heavier taxes on hotels, restaurants, and entertainment make Thailand less of a tourist bargain than in the recent past, and imported goods are always expensive. Still, transport is cheap, especially buses.

Thai and Chinese food can be a great bargain, though foreign ingredients, cooking styles, and decor raise the price considerably. The worst blow in restaurants is the price of wine, but Thai beer and even undistinguished local whisky are inexpensive.

Bargaining. Many foreigners feel uncomfortable with it, but bargaining over prices is customary in several areas of Thai life. For instance, the prices in almost all taxis (except those clearly labelled meter taxis) are negotiated in advance. More protracted bargaining takes place when shopping for souvenirs and in other aspects of commerce; even hotels sometimes have flexible rates. The squeamish can either accept the first price mentioned (which would astound a market trader) or take a fixed-price hotel taxi to one of the big department stores, where the price tags mean business.

PLANNING YOUR BUDGET

To give an idea of what to expect, here are some average prices in Thai baht (Bt). They are only approximate, as inflation takes its toll.

Airport. Limousine service to city centre: Bt500–650. Airport departure tax: international flights Bt500, domestic flights Bt30.

Boats. Long-tailed boats and motorized river boats around Bt300 per hour (negotiable); private two-hour canal cruise Bt500 per boat.

Buses. City buses Bt2.5–3.5, air-conditioned buses Bt6–16 within city boundary. Air-conditioned coach Bangkok–Pattaya (one way) Bt60 (private operators, pick-up from major hotels). Air-conditioned coach Bangkok–Phuket (one way) Bt600 (private operators).

Car hire/car rental (international company). Toyota Corolla 1300/Nissan Sunny 1200 Bt1,700 per day; Bt10,000 per week, unlimited mileage.

Entertainment. Nightclub entry, two drinks, and a floor show Bt200.

Guided tours. Floating market morning tour Bt300. All-day river excursion to Ayutthaya (with lunch) Bt900.

Hairdressers (in top hotels). Women's haircut Bt500, shampoo and set Bt200. Man's haircut Bt400, shave Bt100, shampoo Bt150-200.

Hotels (air-conditioned double room with bath). Budget Bt500–1,000, Tourist Bt1,000–2,000, First class Bt2,500–4,000. Luxury Bt4,000 and up. Add 10 percent service charge and 10 percent V.A.T. (Value-Added Tax). These rates are for peak months (December–March), and are considerably less at other times.

Meals and drinks. Hotel breakfast Bt150-300, lunch Bt300, dinner Bt500, including 10 percent service charge and 10 percent taxes. Beer (local) Bt50, wine (imported) at least Bt350 per bottle.

Taxis. Bt35-80 in central Bangkok (hotel taxis cost twice as much). Taxi-meter: the fare is 35 Baht for a distance of no more than 2 km (1¼ mile). The fare will increase according to distance covered.

Trains. Fares are strictly according to distance, with supplements of Bt30 to 70 for different types of train, Bt50 for air-conditioning, Bt100–520 for a couchette; e.g., Bangkok–Chiang Mai: first class, one way Bt537, return Bt1,074; second class, one way Bt255.

NEWSPAPERS and MAGAZINES

Bangkok has five English-language dailies, *Bangkok Post*, *The Nation*, *Thailand Times, Asia Times,* and *Business Day* to complement its big range of Thai and Chinese papers. Newspapers from elsewhere in Asia and Europe are sold in the major hotels and bookshops. English-language magazines and paperback books are also available.

OPENING HOURS

Banks: 8:30am–3:30pm, Monday to Friday. In seaside tourist areas, most banks operate a foreign-exchange service for tourists until 7:30pm, seven days a week.

Department stores: around 9:30am–9:00pm (or 10pm in Bangkok), seven days a week. Hours are extended at Christmas, New Year, and Chinese New Year.

Government offices: 8:30am–noon and 1–4:30pm, from Monday to Friday.

Museums: around 9am–noon and 1–4:30 pm, every day except Monday and Tuesday.

Post offices: Bangkok's General Post Office is open 24 hours daily.

Chief district post offices 8am–7pm, Monday to Friday and 8am–1pm weekends and holidays. Other offices open 8am–5:30pm Monday to Friday, 8am–12pm Saturday.

Small shops: early morning until 8 or 9pm, often seven days a week.

PHOTOGRAPHY and VIDEO

The golden spires, blue skies, green fields, and lush flowers of Thailand cry out to be photographed. Standard brands and sizes of film are easily available. You can have your pictures processed in one hour (express service) or five hours (standard service). Developed film can also be sent home at "small package" rates. The best camera/film shop in Bangkok is AV Camera on Silom Road.

A special show consisting of classical dancing, sword fighting, and Thai boxing is staged for photographers on Thursday and Sunday mornings at the Oriental Hotel. There are many other opportunities for filming these distinctive pageants, but only here are the conditions so good.

One word of warning: resist any temptation to take "trick" pictures of Buddha statues and other religious objects, or even isolated, dilapidated archaeological relics. For instance, never pose anyone touching a statue. Outraged Thais might accuse you of gross disrespect, however unintended. You should check with your guide if you intend to take pictures in temples or other religious places.

Video. Filming in the Grand Palace is restricted, and in some temples an additional charge is made for the use of video cameras.

POLICE

A special force of Thai Tourist Police operates in crucial areas of Bangkok, such as near tourist attractions and major hotels. Over 100 officers, all of them linguists, stand ready to protect or advise foreigners. They wear the beige military-style uniform of ordinary Thai police with "Tourist Police" shoulder patches.

POST OFFICES (See also OPENING HOURS)

Branch offices are scattered throughout Bangkok and, for the convenience of visitors, can also be found at Don Muang airport. Major hotels also provide postal services.

Mail. You can send letters and postcards airmail, which arrive within four days to a week in North America or Europe. Almost all the big hotels offer basic mailing services, and many newspaper shops sell stamps.

Thailand

Telegrams. Branch post offices accept telegrams, but for round-the-clock cable and telex service go to the telecommunications department on the ground floor of the General Post Office on New Road.

PUBLIC HOLIDAYS

Since many Thai holidays are fixed to the lunar calendar, the dates vary from year to year. Banks and government offices close on these days, but daily life is not necessarily disrupted. The only notable exception to this is Chinese New Year, which is not a public holiday in Thailand, but a time when most businesses close.

1 January	New Year's Day
6 April	Chakri Day, honouring Rama I
13 April	Songkran Day (Water Festival)
1 May	Labour Day
5 May	Coronation Day
12 August	H.M. Queen's Birthday
23 October	Chulalongkorn Day, honouring Rama V
5 December	HM King's Birthday and National Day
10 December	Constitution Day
31 December	New Year's Eve

Movable dates

	Chinese New Year (partly observed)
Maka Puja	Commemoration of meeting at which the Buddha preached the doctrines of Buddhism.
Visakha Puja	Celebrates the birth, Enlightenment, and death of the Buddha. Most holy of Buddhist ceremonial days.
Khao Phansa	First day of Buddhist Lent

R

RADIO and TELEVISION

Television. Four Bangkok TV channels broadcast in colour and black-and-white. Many programmes are foreign shows, mostly American, which are dubbed into Thai. These days, an increasing number of hotels have cable satellite television.

Radio. Bangkok's English-language radio stations can be found on FM 95.5Mhz and 105.5Mhz. These stations offer music interspersed with hourly bulletins. Reception for BBC and Voice of America short-wave programmes is best in the morning or at night. There is also extensive short-wave programming through Radio Beijing and Radio Japan.

RELIGION

In Thailand, more than 90 percent of the population are Theravada Buddhists, but Muslim (especially in southern Thailand), Christian, Hindu, and other faiths are well represented. For foreign visitors, Protestant and Catholic services in Bangkok are advertised in Saturday's editions of the *Bangkok Post*.

T

TELEPHONES

Public telephones are located in post offices throughout the country, and most of them offer a 24-hour international service. Hotels, railway stations, airports, and department stores may also have telephone booths. Most international calls can be dialled direct or made through the operator (dial 100), by placing them through either the telecommunications department or your hotel switchboard (most big hotels normally add a hefty surcharge to international calls). Within Thailand you need to be careful how you read telephone numbers. The hyphen, as in 7010-20, is used by the Thais to indicate all numbers in between 10 and 20, not 10 or 20. We have used a stroke to indicate alternative numbers (i.e. 10/20) and "up to" to indicate all numbers in between (i.e., 10 up to 20).

Thailand

Useful Telephone Numbers

Airport		535 1111
Bangkok Railway		223 0341, 223 7010/20
Bus Station	Northern Terminal	272 5299
	Eastern Terminal	391 2504
	Southern Terminal	435 1199
Directory of Assistance		13 (Bangkok)
Tourism Authority of Thailand		226 0060, 0072, 0085, 0098

Tourist Police   221 6206 up to 10 or 1699 (Bangkok)

Immigration Office 287 3101 up to 10

For lists of hospitals and other emergency services see EMERGENCIES.

TIME DIFFERENCES

Although Thailand has officially adopted the Western 12-month calendar, the traditional lunar calendar is used for ceremonies and everyday activities. Major festivals usually fall in a full-moon period. Another difference: dates are calculated from the year Buddha was born (543 b.c.). For instance, the year 2523 b.e. (Buddhist Era) in Thailand corresponds to our year 1980.

Thailand time year-round is G.M.T. plus 7 hours. The following chart shows the time in January in some selected cities.

New York	London	**Bangkok**	Sydney
midnight	5am	**noon**	4pm

TIPPING

In simple, native-style restaurants and snack bars tipping is not customary. It is better to tip nothing at all than to leave a one-baht tip, which is considered an insult. Taxi drivers are not normally tipped. Further guidance is detailed below:

Barber	10%
Hairdresser	10%
Hotel maid, per week	Bt100
Lavatory attendant	Bt10
Porter	Bt20
Tourist guide	15% (optional)
Waiter	10%

TOILETS

Try to find a hotel or restaurant. In luxury establishments the toilets may have an attendant, in which case a tip is appropriate. Away from the main centres, you will encounter Eastern-style, hole-in-the-floor-type toilets. In places without running water, you will always find a huge jar of water nearby. Scoop water out for flushing and washing.

Where are the toilets?   **hong nam yu ti nai?**

TOURIST INFORMATION OFFICES

The Tourism Authority of Thailand (T.A.T.) operates an information stand in the arrivals hall of Bangkok's Don Muang international airport. You can also obtain leaflets, maps, and advice on the main floor of the organization's head office:

Tourism Authority of Thailand, Head Office, Bamrung 372 Muang Road, Bangkok 10100; tel. 226 0060, 226 0072, 226 0085, 226 0098, 8:30am to 4:30pm daily.

At the same address you'll find the Tourist Assistance Centre, which can provide help in all situations. Telephone 281 5051 or 282 8129, 8:30am to 4:30pm daily. Branch offices of T.A.T. at Chiang Mai, Kanchanaburi, Nakhon Ratchasima (Korat), Pattaya, Hat Yai, and Phuket have useful regional information and maps. In Chiang Mai the address is: 105/1 Chiang Mai-Lamphun Road; tel. 248 604.

Overseas representatives of the Tourism Authority of Thailand can be found in the following countries:

Thailand

Australia: Level 2, National Australia Bank House, 255 George Street, Sydney 2000 NSW; tel. (02) 247 7549/247 7540; fax (02) 251 2465.

United Kingdom: 49 Albemarle Street, London WIX 3FE; tel. (171) 499 7679; fax (171) 629-5519.

U.S.A.: 5 World Trade Center, Suite 3443, New York, NY 10048; tel. (212) 432-0433/0435; fax (212) 912-0920

TOUTS

In Bangkok and, to a lesser extent, in the larger provincial towns of Thailand, tourists are often pestered by touts, black marketeers, and pimps. Some are charmingly convincing, others obnoxiously persistent. The best course is to smile and walk away. If you want a bona fide guide, ask a travel agency (see Guides and Tours). If you need advice about shopping, ask the Tourism Authority of Thailand for their Official Shopping Guide booklet.

TRANSPORT

PUBLIC TRANSPORT

Buses. A well-developed network of city buses serves Bangkok. Fares are very low and service is as good as can be reasonably expected in a traffic-jammed metropolis. Though some of the buses are old and cramped, the new air-conditioned models (for a premium fare along special routes) meet high standards. If you plan to cut your expenses by using buses instead of taxis, invest in one of the Bangkok street maps which show the routes. All city buses have route numbers marked in arabic numerals, but destinations are written in Thai. You don't pay as you get on to a city bus; the conductor, jingling a coin box, will come round to sell you a fixed-fare ticket.

Inter-city coaches range from rickety veterans to comfortable air-conditioned cruisers, and prices vary accordingly. On the heavily travelled routes, like Bangkok to Pattaya, luxury coaches operated by various companies make frequent departures.

Where's the bus stop? **pai rod may yu ti nai?**

Trains. Although the competing air-conditioned buses often travel faster, Thailand's state railway system provides an efficient means of seeing the country. A train is, after all, an adventure, no less so when amongst a crowd of friendly Thai travellers. There are reasonably luxurious air-conditioned first-class cars, comfortable second-class accommodation (including couchettes, which can be reserved), and old-fashioned, wooden third-class cars. Travel agents, hotel desks, and the information office at the main (Hualampong) railway station can advise you on schedules and fares. Bangkok's main stations are:

Hualampong on Rama IV Road — for the north and northeast and for express trains to the south.

Makkasan on Nikom Makkasan Road — for the east.

Thon Buri on Bangkok Noi, Rod Fai Road — for the slower trains to the south.

Telephone 223 7010/20 for general information on rail travel.

TAXIS AND SAMLORS

Taxis. In Bangkok you don't have to whistle for a taxi — just look at one and the driver will jam on the brakes. Taxis are so plentiful that they can be a nuisance, and drivers congregate near hotels and cruise alongside strolling foreigners to solicit business.

Until recently, although virtually all Bangkok taxis had meters, they almost never used them. These days a new, smarter breed of taxi has emerged with a big sign saying "TAXI-METER." If you cannot find one of these and opt for an older model, remember that you must haggle over the fare before getting into the cab. Once agreed, the price is a matter of honour; no tip is expected. To make things easier, ask your hotel receptionist to write down your destination in Thai so you can show it to the driver, since foreigners' pronunciation of street or place names is rarely understood. The hotel receptionist should also be able to advise you what the appropriate fare will be. This depends on the distance and the amount of traffic.

If you can't stand the haggling and the language problem, you can take an air-conditioned hotel taxi. The fares are set, and are usually at least twice what a public taxi would cost, but they have the advantage that drivers very often know some English.

Even some of the larger provincial towns have no conventional taxis at all. You can take a *samlor* or, for longer trips, hail an empty mini-bus. In either case, be sure you agree on the fare in advance.

Samlors/Tuk-Tuks. Useful and adventurous for short trips, these noisy little three-wheeled motorbikes nip in and out of Bangkok's traffic. Samlors cost a few baht less than four-wheeled taxis and should always be subject to negotiation before you sit down.

W

WATER

Don't drink the tap water in Thailand. Most hotels place a bottle or flask of purified water in every room. Responsible restaurants serve bottled water and pure ice, but be cautious about the ice in drinks at roadside stands. To be on the safe side in questionable situations, insist on bottled water or soft drinks and beer without ice.

a bottle of drinking water **nam yen nung khuad**

WEIGHTS and MEASURES

Thailand adopted the metric system more than 50 years ago, but a few traditional measures still exist. The one most frequently seen is the rai: 1 rai = 0.4 acres (0.16 hectares).

For fluid and distance measures see DRIVING.

Length

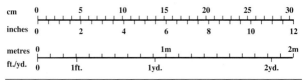

Weight

grams	0	100	200	300	400	500	600	700	800	900	1kg
ounces	0		4		8		12		1lb		20		24		28		2lb

Temperature

| °C | | -30 | -25 | -20 | -15 | -10 | -5 | 0 | 5 | 10 | 15 | 20 | 25 | 30 | 35 | 40 | 45 |
| °F | | -20 | | -10 | | 0 | | 10 | | 20 | | 30 | | 40 | | 50 | | 60 | | 70 | | 80 | | 90 | | 100 | | 110 |

Y

YOUTH HOSTELS

Thailand has a few youth hostels; refer to Hostelling International (published by the International Youth Federation). Bangkok also has a YMCA (27 Sathorn Thai Road; tel. 286 5134) and a YWCA (13 Sathorn Thai Road; tel. 286 1936). Many Bangkok hotels offer student discounts.

SOME USEFUL EXPRESSIONS

Numbers

one	**neuhng**	fifteen	**sip-har**
two	**sorng**	sixteen	**sip-hok**
three	**sarm**	seventeen	**sip-jeht**
four	**see**	eighteen	**sip-(b)pairt**
five	**har**	nineteen	**sip-gow**
six	**hok**	twenty	**yee-sip**
seven	**jeht**	thirty	**sarm-sip**
eight	**(b)pairt**	forty	**see-sip**
nine	**gow**	fifty	**har-sip**
ten	**sip**	sixty	**hok-sip**
eleven	**sip-eht**	seventy	**jeht-sip**
twelve	**sip-sorng**	eighty	**(b)pairt-sip**
thirteen	**sip-sarm**	ninety	**gow-sip**
fourteen	**sip-see**	hundred	**roy**

Thailand

Days of the Week

Sunday	**wan ar tit**	Thursday	**wan pa ru hat**
Monday	**wan jan**	Friday	**wan suk**
Tuesday	**wan ang karn**	Saturday	**wan sow**
Wednesday	**wan put**		

yesterday/today/tomorrow	**mua wan ni/wan ni/prung ni**
day/week/month/year	**wan/sap da/duan/pi**
left/right	**sai/khwa**
up/down	**bon/lang**
good/bad	**dee/lehw**
big/small	**yai/lehk**
cheap/expensive	**took/pairng**
hot/cold	**rorn/yehn**
old/new	**gow/mai**
early/late	**chow/sai**
easy/difficult	**ngai/yark**
heavy/light	**nak/bow**
here/there	**tee nee/tee nan**
next/last	**nar/tee laiw**
quick/slow	**rehw/char**
When does ... open/close?	**... pert/pit meua rai?**
What's the fare to ...?	**(b)pai ... kit tow rai?**
Could you speak more slowly?	**poot char long noy day mai?**

Recommended Hotels

Below is a selection of hotels listed according to town or area, alphabetically. Prices will vary according to the season in which you visit, travel agent's package, and unpredictable inflation. All the hotels included have air-conditioning. The following symbols are a basic guide to room prices (based on double occupancy with bath, but not including breakfast):

✪	Bt500–1,000 (Budget)
✪✪	Bt1,000–2,000 (Tourist)
✪✪✪	Over Bt2,000 (First Class)

BANGKOK LOCAL DIALLING CODE (02)

Comfort Inn ✪ *153/11 Sukhumvit Road, Soi 11; Tel. 251 9250; fax 254 3562.* Modern, no-frills hotel with fairly small rooms and a quiet but central location.

Dusit Thani ✪✪✪ *946 Rama IV Road; Tel. 236 0450; fax 236 6400.* One of Bangkok's most luxurious and tasteful hotels, offering excellent restaurants, swimming pool, and all the high-quality services you'd expect from a top-rated establishment. 525 rooms.

Federal Hotel ✪ *27 Soi 11, Sukhumvit Road; Tel. 253 0175/6; fax 253 5322.* Welcoming, modern hotel with a swimming pool, patio, and coffee shop. 80 rooms.

Impala Hotel ✪✪ *9 Soi 24, Sukhumvit Road; Tel. 259 0053/4; fax 258 8747.* Situated a little bit away from it all, and offering a swimming pool, sauna, and health club amongst its facilities. 200 rooms.

Malaysia Hotel ✪ *54 Rama IV Soi Ngam Dupli, Rama IV Road; Tel. 286 3582; fax 249 3120.* Something like an upscale backpackers' paradise, complete with a nearby pool and notorious 24-hour coffee shop. 120 rooms.

Manohra Hotel ✪✪ *412 Surawong Road; Tel. 234 5070 up to 88; fax 237 7662.* Situated within walking distance of the Chao

Phraya River. All rooms have recently been renovated and there is an indoor swimming pool, cocktail lounge, and pleasant roof garden. 250 rooms.

Menam Hotel ✪✪✪ *2074 Charoen Krung Road, Yannawa; Tel. 289 1148/9 or 289 0352/3; fax 291 1048.* The least expensive and most unpretentious of the riverside hotels, with a swimming pool, health club, and terraces. 727 rooms.

Opera Hotel ✪ *16 Soi 1, Phetchburi Road; Tel. 252 4031/2.* Cheap, cheerful, and popular, with pool and 24-hour coffee shop.

Oriental Hotel ✪✪✪ *48 Oriental Avenue, Charoen Krung Road; Tel. 236 0400/0420; fax 236 1937.* Nominated as one of the world's finest hotels, with two swimming pools, a host of famous clients, and fine views of the river. 394 rooms.

Park Hotel ✪✪ *6 Soi 7, Sukhumvit Road; Tel. 255 4300, 252 5110/3; fax 255 4309.* Recently refurbished with swimming pool, fitness centre, sauna, and jacuzzi. 139 rooms.

Royal Hotel ✪✪ *2 Ratchadamnoen Klang Road; Tel. 222 9111/20; fax 224 2083.* One of Bangkok's venerable old institutions, positioned close to the famous Grand Palace. 300 rooms.

Shangri-La Hotel ✪✪✪ *89 Soi Wat Suan Plu, Charoen Krung Road; Tel. 236 7777; fax 236 8579.* A luxury establishment known for superb river views and fine restaurants, and which offers a pool and top-class service. 694 rooms.

YMCA Collins International House ✪✪ *27 Sathornrai Road; Tel. 287 1900; fax 287 1996.* Clean, friendly accommodation of a high standard, with a good-value restaurant and adjacent swimming pool. 50 rooms.

CHIANG MAI LOCAL DIALLING CODE (053)

Chiang Mai Orchid ✪✪✪ *100 Huey Kaew Road; Tel. 222 099/222 091/3; fax 221 625.* One of Chiang Mai's best establishments, with a swimming pool, fitness centre, nightclub, and lively disco. 450 rooms.

Chiang Mai Plaza ✪✪✪ *92 Sri Donchai Road; Tel. 270 036/050; fax 272 230.* Offering all the facilities of a top international-class hotel and the convenience of a downtown location, with a large swimming pool and a popular discotheque. 450 rooms.

Galare Guest House ✪ *7/1 Charoenprathet Road Soi 2; Tel. 249 088; fax 277 088;* An upscale guesthouse in a charming location overlooking the river, a short walk from town. 30 rooms.

Holiday Garden Hotel ✪✪ *16/16 Huey Kaew Road; Tel. 210 901; fax 210 905.* Located in downtown Chiang Mai, this peaceful family hotel is positioned around a courtyard with a swimming pool.

Hotel Top North Centre ✪ *15 Moonmuang Soi 2 Road; Tel. 213 900.* Popular middle-of-the-road hotel, situated in a quiet cul-de-sac off Tapei Gate and within easy walk of a number of bars and temples.

Lai Thai Guest House ✪ *111/4–5 Kotchasan Road; Tel. 271 725; fax 272 724.* A clean and modern chalet-style hotel built around a courtyard, and with friendly staff. 90 rooms.

Once Upon a Time ✪✪ *385/2 Charoenprathet Road; Tel. 274 932.* This hotel provides eccentric wooden rooms and is situated in beautifully exotic gardens.

Rim Ping Garden ✪✪✪ *411 Charoenprathet Road; Tel. 281 059/60.* In an idyllic riverside setting, with a swimming pool, fine restaurant. and balconied rooms. 20 rooms.

River View Lodge ✪ *25 Soi 2, Charoenprathet Road; Tel. 271 110; fax 281 044.* Charming riverbank setting, with large garden and fine views. 36 rooms.

Royal Princess Hotel ✪✪✪ *112 Chang Klan Road; Tel. 281 033; fax 281 044.* Bright and elegant, with a swimming pool. Central location near the night market. 200 rooms.

CHIANG RAI Local dialling code (053)

Dusit Island Resort ✪✪✪ *1129 Kraisorasit Road; Tel. 715 777; fax 715 801.* Big international hotel with fine views over the river and of facilities.

Golden Triangle Inn ✪✪ *590 Phahonyothin Road; Tel. 711 339; fax 713 963.* In a quiet location near the heart of town. Charming staff and an excellent café.

Maekok Villa ✪ *445 Singhakai Road; Tel. 711 786.* Charming bungalow-style rooms with bath and hot water, situated on the edge of town. 44 rooms.

Rimkok Resort ✪✪✪ *6 Mu 4, Tha Thon Road; Tel. 716 445/60; fax 715 859.* Massive hotel complex with jogging facilities, pool, and fine river views. Sited approximately 5 km (3 miles) from town. 248 rooms.

Wang Din Place ✪✪ *34/1 Kwae Wai Road; Tel. 713 363.* Twelve comfortable riverside huts, 2 km (1 mile) from town.

YMCA ✪ *70 Phahonyothin Road; Tel. 713 785; fax 714 336.* Modern establishment on the outskirts of town. Swimming pool.

HAT YAI LOCAL DIALLING CODE (074)

JB Hotel ✪✪✪ *99 Juti Anusorn Road; Tel. 234 300 up to 18; Tel. Bangkok 238 4790; fax Bangkok 238 4797.* Tastefully decorated hotel with a swimming pool, tennis court, and health club. 212 rooms.

Prince Hotel ✪ *138 Thamnounvithi Road; Tel. 243 160.* Down-to-earth hotel in a central location, with coffee shop.

Regency Hotel ✪✪ *23 Prachathipat Road; Tel. 234 400 up to 9; fax 234 515.* Elegantly furnished in a central location, but without swimming pool. 190 rooms.

HUA HIN LOCAL DIALLING CODE (032)

Hua Hin Highland Resort ✪✪ *4/15 Ban Samopong Hua Hin; Tel. 512 487.* Situated to the north of town, near the golf course. 13 rooms.

Royal Garden Resort ✪✪✪ *107/1 Phetkasem Road; Tel. 511 881/4; fax 512 422.* Offering a swimming pool, roof terrace, tennis courts, and even a view of the sea from every one of its 217 rooms.

Sailom ✪✪ *29 Phetkasem Road; Tel. 511 890/1; fax 512 047.* A popular upscale hotel with a swimming pool and tennis courts. 60 rooms.

Sofitel Central ✪✪✪ *1 Damnoen Kasem Road; Tel. 512 021/30; fax 511 014.* A charming, colonial-style hotel positioned right on the beachfront and recently renovated to the highest standards. 218 rooms.

KANCHANABURI Local dialling code (034)

Kasem Island Resort ✪ *27 Chaichumphon Road; Tel. 511 359.* A selection of chalet-style rooms situated in a good location on an island in the Mae Klong River — only a stone's throw away from Kanchanaburi town.

Pung Waan Resort ✪✪ *123/1 Tarsao, Sai Yok, Kanchanaburi; Tel. 591 017/8; fax 591 017.* A choice of either floating houses or brick huts situated a short way out of Kanchanaburi, and offering their own extensive and beautiful landscaped gardens, as well as a swimming pool.

River Kwai Hotel ✪✪ *284/3–16 Saeng Chuto Road; Tel. 511 184; fax 511 269.* Centrally located, with a restaurant and swimming pool, but no views of the river. 127 rooms.

River Kwai Village ✪✪ *72 Mu 4, Thasao, Sai Yok, Kanchanaburi; Tel 591 055; Tel. Bangkok 251 7522/7828; fax 591 054.* Situated to the west of town near the Sai Yok National Park, and offering a range of diverse attractions, from a swimming pool and an abundance of package tours to a mini-zoo.

Sam's Place ✪ *Song Kwai Road; Tel. 513 971.* Simple but charming river bungalows situated in a convenient location near Kanchanaburi's main concentration of bars and floating restaurants.

KO SAMUI Local dialling code (077)

Chaweng Garden ✪ *Chaweng Beach; Tel. and fax 422 265.* Pretty bungalows made of wood in an attractive leafy setting, close to the popular centre of Chaweng Beach.

Coral Bay Resort ✪✪ *Bo Phut Beach; Tel. 422 223/4; fax 422 392.* Large, thatched bungalows with spacious balconies, plus a swimming pool and terrace.

Imperial Boat House Hotel ✪✪✪ *Choeng Mong Beach; Tel. 425 041; fax 425 460.* Stunning hotel made up of old teak canal barges converted into luxury, land-based suites.

Imperial Ko Samui ✪✪✪ *Chaweng Beach; Tel. 422 020; fax 422 396/7.* International-class hotel, charmingly situated in a secluded cove, with beautiful gardens, two swimming pools, and fine views.

Imperial's Tong Sai Bay Hotel ✪✪✪ *Choeng Mong Beach; Tel. 425 015; fax 425 462.* International-class hotel built on the cliffs with balconies, tennis court, private beach, swimming pool, and spectacular views.

The Island ✪✪ *Chaweng Beach; Tel. 230 941; fax 230 942.* Thatched bungalows, bar, restaurant, and swimming pool, situated on popular Chaweng Beach.

Matlang Resort ✪ *Chaweng Beach; Tel. 422 172; fax 422 172.* At the quieter, northern end of Chaweng, set in a pretty garden.

PS Villa ✪ *Choeng Mong Beach; Tel. 425 161; fax 425 403.* Clean and friendly, with fine views; situated on a quiet beach.

Sandy Resort ✪ *Bo Phut Beach; Tel. 425 353/4.* Inland bungalows with charming wooden terraces.

MAE HONG SON LOCAL DIALLING CODE (053)

Baiyoke Chalet ✪✪ *90 Khunlumprapas Road; Tel. 611 486; fax 611 533.* Upscale and with a central location, this chalet-style hotel offers cosy rooms and a restaurant.

Holiday Inn ✪✪✪ *114/5–7 Khunlumprapas Road; Tel. 612 324; fax 611 524.* Big international-class hotel with a swimming pool, disco, bars, and convention facilities. 114 rooms.

Imperial Tara Mae Hong Son ✪✪✪ *149 Mu 8; Tel. 611 473; fax 611 252.* Five-star luxury hotel in extensive landscaped gardens, with charming views. Full facilities, including restaurants and swimming pool.

Mae Hong Son Resort ✪ *24 Ban Huey Dua; Tel. 611 406; fax 251 135.* Charming bungalows located 5 km (3 miles) outside Mae Hong Son. 40 bungalows available.

Rim Nam Klang Doi Resort ✪✪ *Ban Huay Dua; Tel. 611 142; fax 611 086.* Standard and luxury huts on the river bank, 5 km (3 miles) out of town, with a restaurant terrace and friendly staff.

PATTAYA LOCAL DIALLING CODE (038)

Amari Orchid Lodge ✪✪ *Beach Road; Tel. 428 175.* Well-appointed hotel overlooking Beach Road with a swimming pool, terrace, and many bars and restaurants nearby.

Diana Inn ✪ *216/6–9 Mu 9, Pattaya 2 Road; Tel. 429 675; fax 424 566.* Pleasant little hotel with a swimming pool, conveniently situated near the centre of town. 59 rooms.

Dusit Resort ✪✪✪ *240/2 Beach Road; Tel. 425 611 up to 21; fax 428 239.* International-class hotel with good service and a wide choice of facilities, including a swimming pool, tennis courts, and an opulent bar for evening drinks. 500 rooms.

Garden Lodge ✪ *170 Mu 5, Naklua Soi 12; Tel. 429 109.* Swimming pool and breakfast buffet. 58 rooms.

PK Villa ✪✪ *Beach Road; Tel. 429 107.* Always one of Pattaya's most popular establishments, set in a villa with well-tended gardens and a swimming pool.

Royal Cliff Beach ✪✪✪ *Cliff Road, South Pattaya; Tel. 250 421 up to 430; fax 250 511 or 250 513.* Considered by most to be the best hotel in town, with its own private beach, swimming pools, restaurants, and exquisite views. 700 rooms.

Seaview Resort ✪✪ *Naklua Soi 18; Tel. 429 317; fax 423 668.* Situated away from it all, a short distance from North Pattaya, with a private beach, good water for swimming, and restaurant. 80 cottages.

Siam Bayshore ✪✪✪ *Beach Road; Tel. and fax 428 677 up to 79.* Luxury hotel set in 8 hectares (20 acres) of woods and lovely tropical gardens, in a good location just a short walk from the busiest area of town. 265 rooms.

PHUKET LOCAL DIALLING CODE (076)

Amanpuri ✪✪✪ *118 Srisoonthorn Road, Pansea Beach; Tel. 324 333 up to 38; fax 324 100 or 324 200.* Phuket's finest hotel, with exclusive bungalows overlooking a secluded bay.

Offering a swimming pool, tennis courts, and a private cruiser. 40 rooms.

Boathouse Inn ✪✪✪ *Kata Beach; Tel. 330 015 up to 17; fax 330 561.* A charming inn modelled on traditional Thai boathouses, offering a swimming pool, a good restaurant, and beachfront location.

Casuarina Bungalows ✪✪✪ *Patong Beach; Tel. 340 123.* Simple bungalows attractively set in pretty gardens, in a convenient location for Phuket's busiest and most exciting beach area.

Club Andaman ✪✪ *77/1 Patong Beach; Tel. 340 530; fax 342 123.* Thai-style thatched bungalows, with a swimming pool and extensive landscaped gardens, near busy Patong.

Jungle Beach Resort ✪✪ *11/3 Vised Road, Nai Harn; Tel. 381 108 or 288 341.* Attractively set in its own rocky bay, with swimming pool and terrace, in one of the less developed areas of the island. 38 rooms.

Pansea Phuket Bay ✪✪✪ *Pansea Beach; Tel. 324 017/020.* Luxurious thatched bungalows on stilts, plus a swimming pool, fine restaurant, good service, bars, terrace, and private beach. 100 rooms.

Patong Beach Bungalow ✪✪ *96/1 Patong Beach; Tel. 340 117.* Close to busy Patong, small swimming pool plus a beachfront terrace. 34 rooms.

Sunset Bungalows ✪ *Nai Harn Beach.* Old-style beach bungalows situated up a hillside in one of the least-developed parts of the island.

Recommended Restaurants

Below is a selection of some of the eating establishments that have made Thailand a gastronomic delight, and in which we appreciate the food and service; if you find other places worth recommending, we would be pleased to hear from you. Our choices concentrate mainly on restaurants serving local cuisine, rather than international or Western. Some establishments close one day a week, which may vary, so it's often best to telephone ahead. Alternatively, just watch where the locals go and take your pick. You're unlikely to be disappointed.

Apart from the more expensive hotel restaurants, average meal prices (two dishes, rice, and dessert) are fairly uniform — ranging from roughly Bt100 to Bt400 per adult. Beer is extra, of course, while wine for the most part is extremely expensive, sometimes even costing more than the meal. Restaurant opening hours are usually 11am–2pm and 6–10pm; some remain open all day. The following symbols are a guide to prices:

✪	cheap
✪✪	medium
✪✪✪	expensive

BANGKOK

Baan Khanitha ✪✪ *36/1 Soi 23, Sukhumvit; Tel. 258 4181.* High-quality Thai cuisine in an elegant traditional Thai house.

Baan Thai ✪✪ *7 Soi 32, Sukhumvit Road; Tel. 258 5403.* A diverse selection of Thai dishes modified for the Western palate, accompanied by classical dancing. Nightly performances are from 7:30 to 10pm.

Ban Khun Por ✪✪ *Siam Square Soi 8; Tel. 250 1252.* Well-prepared classic Thai cuisine served in beautiful antique decor. Popular with foreign residents and Thai yuppies.

Ban Krua ✪✪ *29/1 Soi Saladaeng 1, Silom Road; Tel. 233 6912.* Simple but comfortable restaurant, with good local specialities on the menu.

Bussaracum ✪✪✪ *35 Soi 2 Piphat, Convent Road; Tel. 235 8915 or 266 6312.* Authentic Thai cuisine, featuring *sakunna chom suan* (shrimp birds with taro).

Cabbages and Condoms ✪✪✪ *10 Soi 12, Sukhumvit Road; Tel. 229 4610.* Organic Thai cuisine.

The China House ✪✪✪ *Oriental Hotel, 48 Oriental Avenue; Tel. 236 0400.* Bangkok's first and finest classic Cantonese restaurant, situated in an elegant wooden house. The excellent food includes shark's fin soup and roast pigeon stuffed with herbs. This restaurant is expensive compared to normal Bangkok standards.

Jade Garden ✪✪ *Montien Hotel, 54 Surawong Road; Tel. 233 7060.* Popular Cantonese cuisine, particularly the *dim sum*, as well as delicious noodles, steamed dumplings, and Peking duck.

La Banane ✪✪ *99/24 Langsuan Balcony, Ploenchit Road; Tel. 251 9822.* Friendly atmosphere. Good value Thai cuisine with an emphasis on seafood.

Lemongrass ✪✪ *5/1 Soi 24, Sukhumvit Road; Tel. 258 8637.* Delightful old house with charming terrace. Excellent Thai food, but the portions are small.

Loy Nava Dinner Cruise ✪✪ *Oriental Ferry; Tel. 437 4932.* Departs every evening for a dinner cruise on Chao Phraya River. Serves good Western and European food. Advance booking recommended.

Madame Cherie ✪ *Charn Issara Tower, Rama IV Road; Tel. 234 2211.* Popular Vietnamese cuisine near Bangkok's red-light district.

Royal India Restaurant ✪ *392/1 Chakraphet Road; Tel. 221 6565.* Small and extremely popular, with fine tandooris, Madras curries, and Indian sweets.

Sala Rim Naam Oriental Hotel ✪✪✪ *48 Oriental Avenue, Charoen Krung Road; Tel. 437 6211*. Set in a charming location on the banks of the Chao Phraya River, with exquisite classical dancing every night (at 8:30pm). Serving some of the best — and most expensive — Thai food to be found in the city.

Seafood Market and Restaurant ✪✪✪ *388 Sukhumvit Road; Tel. 281 2071/5*. Choose your seafood in a shopping trolley, then sit outside and feast on some of the best fish and lobster in town. Meals here can be very expensive.

See Fah ✪✪ *Siam Square Soi 11; Tel. 251 5517; also has branches at 47/19-22 Ratchodamri Road; Thaniya Road; Sukhumvit Soi 55; and 1911 Ramkamhaeng Road*. Big, bright, well-frequented chain restaurant serving popular Chinese dishes at moderate prices. Speedy service.

Silom Village ✪ *286 Silom Road; Tel. 234 4448*. Fresh fish, Chinese, and Thai specialities served at both open-air and indoor restaurants, to the accompaniment of Thai music.

Spice Market ✪✪✪ *The Regent Hotel, 155 Ratchadamri Road; Tel. 251 6127*. Captures the feel of old Siam with fine seafoods, green curries, and spicy *tom yam*.

Thanying Restaurant ✪✪ *10 Pramuan Street, off Silom Road; Tel. 236 4361*. Beautifully presented Thai food in an upscale and stylish renovated Thai house. Try the wild pork, stir-fried with lesser galangal and basil, or the duck curry.

Tum Nak Thai ✪ *131 Ratchadaphisek Road; Tel. 274 6420/22*. The second-largest restaurant in the world, seating up to an astounding 3,000 diners who are attended by 120 chefs and 400 waiters on rollerskates! Not surprisingly, service can be poor, but worth a visit for the experience!

Whole Earth ✪✪ *93/3 Soi Lang Suan, Ploenchit Road; Tel. 252 5574*. One of Bangkok's only vegetarian restaurants, also offering a wide selection of non-vegetarian and Thai dishes.

CHIANG MAI

Antique House ✪✪ *71 Charoenprathet Road; Tel. 276 810.*
Thai and European cuisine in teak house with antiques gallery.
Near night bazaar.

Baan Suan ✪✪ *51/3 Chiang Mai Sankamhaeng Road; Tel.*
242 116. Situated in several 100-year-old teakwood barns on the
outskirts of town, serves a wide selection of Thai food.

Diamond Hotel ✪✪✪ *33/10 Charoenprathet Road; Tel. 270*
080 up to 085. A set *khantoke* meal accompanied by traditional
dancing in an old teak house. Book in advance.

Gallery ✪✪ *25–29 Charoen Rat Road; Tel. 248 601.* Delicacies
such as spicy curry and banana flower salad.

Kaiwan Restaurant ✪ *181 Nimanhemin Road; Tel. 221 147.*
Attractively situated on a peaceful veranda. Especially recommended is the *kratongtong* pancake filled with chicken in white
sauce.

La Villa Pizzeria ✪✪ *145 Ratchadamnoen Road; Tel. 277*
*403.*Bright and friendly establishment famed for its seafood pizzas and ravishing antipasti.

Nang Nual ✪✪ *67 Kotchasarn Road, 27 Koa Klang Road,*
Nong Hoy; Tel. 241 771. Ornate and friendly, serving some of
the best seafood in town.

Old Chiang Mai Cultural Centre ✪✪✪ *185/3 Wualai*
Road; Tel. 275 097. A set *khantoke* dinner, including specialities
such as *nam prik ong* (minced pork with chillies).

Rajawadee Restaurant ✪✪ *411 Charoenprathet Road; Tel.*
281 060. Riverside hotel restaurant specializing in a broad selection of Thai, European, and Chinese dishes.

Riverside ✪✪ *9/11 Charoen Rat Road; Tel. 243 239.*
Particularly popular in the early evening for its views of the river
and later for rock bands, as well as its European and Thai cuisine.

Whole Earth Restaurant ✪✪ *88 Sridonchai Road; Tel. 282 463.* A generous selection of vegetarian, non-vegetarian, Indian, and Thai food is served in this northern-style house. Charming atmosphere.

CHIANG RAI

Dusit Island Café ✪✪ *1129 Kraisorasit; Tel. 715 777.* Here you will find a variety of northern specialities served on a pleasant terrace overlooking the river.

Golden Triangle Café ✪✪ *590 Phahonyothin Road; Tel. 711 339.* Popular and friendly, serving delicious Thai, Chinese, and Western food, and occasionally hosting a folk band.

HAT YAI

Best Kitchen ✪ *53 Juti Anusorn Road; Tel. 234 479.* Bright and popular restaurant, with over 100 dishes on the menu, including a speciality of curried wild boar.

Hillman Restaurant ✪✪ *154–8 Niphat Uthit 3 Road; Tel. 244 333.* Particularly famous for its roast suckling pig and lemon chicken.

KO SAMUI

Imperial Samui Restaurant ✪✪ *Imperial Samui Hotel, Chaweng Beach; Tel. 422 020.* Delightfully situated, at one of the island's top hotels, with superlative, if expensive, Thai and European cuisine.

Imperial Tongsai Bay Restaurant ✪✪✪ *Imperial Tong Sai Bay Hotel, Ban Plailaem, Bophut; Tel. 425 015.* Regarded by most as the *crème de la crème* of Ko Samui cuisine, with the advantage of being in one of the island's most beautiful settings. A perfect restaurant for celebrations.

PATTAYA

Dolf Riks ✪ *Sri Nakorn Centre, North Pattaya; Tel. 528 586.* One of Pattaya's oldest and best-loved restaurants, serving good-value Indonesian and European food. House speciality is *rijstafel*, a combination of 18 dishes.

El Toro Steak House ✪ *215–31 Pattaya 2 Road; Tel. 426 238.* For good old steaks, chips, and crowds, nothing can beat the El Toro Steak House.

La Gritta ✪✪ *Amari Orchid Lodge, Beach Road; Tel. 428 161.* Popular restaurant serving good, authentic Italian food. Try the pasta with clams, herbs, and white wine. Book early.

Nang Nual ✪✪ *214/10 South Pattaya Beach Road; Tel 428 478.* This excellent seafood restaurant is worth a visit. Well situated right on the waterfront.

Pattaya Seafood Palace ✪✪ *Mu 10; Tel. 427 396.* Good lobster, mussels, and freshly caught fish served in a pleasant setting.

PIC Kitchen ✪✪✪ *Soi 5, Beach Road; Tel. 428 387.* Widely acclaimed; some of the most authentic local Thai cuisine is served here in a charming atmosphere, surrounded by traditional architecture. Do not miss the opportunity to eat here.

Ruen Thai Restaurant ✪✪ *Pattaya 2 Road, South Pattaya; Tel. 425 911.* Set in beautiful gardens, serving fine curries and regional specialities. Meals are accompanied by exquisite classical dancing.

San Domenico's ✪✪✪ *Jomtien Road; Tel. 426 871.* Popular restaurant serving first-class Italian food. Try the buffet, which is an excellent value, and don't miss the selection of superb desserts.

Thang Long ✪ *Soi 3, 201 Pattaya; Tel. 425 487.* Classical Vietnamese food served by waitresses in traditional Vietnamese costumes.

Vientiane Restaurant ✪✪ *485/18 Pattaya 2 Road; Tel. 411 298.* Good restaurant serving a wide range of quality Thai and Laotian dishes.

PHUKET

Amanpuri ✪✪✪ *Amanpuri Hotel, 118 Srisoonthorn Road, Pansea Beach; Tel. 311 394.* One of the best restaurants you'll find on Phuket, serving top-of-the-range Continental cuisine.

Ban Rim Pa ✪✪✪ *100 / 7 Kalim Beach Road; Tel. 340 789.* One of Phuket's finest restaurants, in a beautiful teak house, with excellent duck curry and *tom yam.*

Buffalo Steak House ✪✪ *94/25–26 Soi Patong, Patong Beach; Tel. 340 855.* This restaurant is known for its New Zealand beef steak, Scandinavian and German dishes, and even elephant's ear!

Malee's Seafood Village ✪✪ *94/4 Thawiwong Road, Patong Beach; Tel. 321 205.* Seafood and steaks served in a beautiful indoor garden.

Phuket View Restaurant ✪✪ *Khao Rang Hill; Tel. 216 865.* Serving a wide range of fresh seafood, Thai, and European dishes, and affording fine views.

Pizzeria Holiday Inn ✪✪ *Patong Beach; Tel. 340 608/9.* Pizzas from a wood-fired brick oven served by the pool in the garden.

Ruam Thep Inn ✪ *Karon Beach.* A popular seafood restaurant with a vast menu of Thai, Chinese, and Western dishes.

Seafood Market ✪ *Patong Night Plaza; Tel. 01 723 0566.* Select your own seafood and watch it being cooked exactly to order. Lively atmosphere.

Tung Ka Café ✪✪ *Khao Rang Hill; Tel. 211 500.* Delicious seafood curry served in coconut, glass noodles with crab, and tempura shrimp — all accompanied by awesome views.

Vecchia Venezia ✪✪ *82/16 Raj-U-Thit Road, Patong Beach.* Italian fare with a Thai touch — choose your fish from the viewing tank or try other specialities such as homemade pasta and pizzas.

ABOUT BERLITZ

In 1878 Professor Maximilian Berlitz had a revolutionary idea about making language learning accessible and enjoyable. One hundred and twenty years later these same principles are still successfully at work.

For language instruction, translation and interpretation services, cross-cultural training, study abroad programs, and an array of publishing products and additional services, visit any one of our more than 350 Berlitz Centers in over 40 countries.

Please consult your local telephone directory for the Berlitz Center nearest you or visit our web site at http://www.berlitz.com.

Helping the World Communicate